DATE DUE			
M.H.C. LIBRARY AUG 14 '72			
GAYLORD			PRINTED IN U.S.A.

THE HIDDEN CURRICULUM

THE HIDDEN CURRICULUM

BENSON R. SNYDER, M.D.

Andrew S. Thomas Memorial Library
MORRIS HARVEY COLLEGE, CHARLESTON, W. VA.

Alfred A. Knopf - New York
1971

79453

378
Sn 92h

THIS IS A BORZOI BOOK
PUBLISHED BY ALFRED A. KNOPF, INC.

Copyright © 1970 by Benson R. Snyder

All rights reserved under International and Pan-American Copyright Conventions. Published in the United States by Alfred A. Knopf, Inc., New York, and simultaneously in Canada by Random House of Canada Limited, Toronto. Distributed by Random House, Inc., New York.

Library of Congress Catalog Card Number: 71–118714
Standard Book Number: 394–42842–0

Manufactured in the United States of America

First Edition

to the students
who taught me much
that is in this book

CONTENTS

Foreword   ix
1. The Two Curricula   3
2. Selective Negligence, Competence, and Commitment   29
3. Distraction and the Expropriation of Learning   65
4. Labs and Lawns   100
5. Education for Complexity   123
6. The Ecological Trap   146
7. Epilogue: Ways of Knowing   176

FOREWORD

This book concerns education in a period of rapid and unpredictable change. We are confronted with the necessity of educating students without either the students or their education becoming obsolete. The larger question, one that transcends the university, is how man can accommodate to change and move into the future without completely losing a sense of continuity with the past.

As a student of psychiatry, I was trained to believe that educational institutions were capable of rational responses to new and often irrational circumstances. Yet I saw universities respond, often unintentionally, by ignoring the extent of the impact of change on both their faculty and students. This negligence obviously compromised the institutions' ability for rational response. The long-range effect of one fiscal decision by a dean, a curriculum decision by a faculty committee, or the study habit of a student went largely unexamined by all participants. Both the educational and personal consequences of the lack of

FOREWORD

recognition of such phenomena have dominated my activities over the past decade.

My perspective is primarily ecological and only secondarily psychological. I have tried to study carefully the manner in which men and women accommodate to major shifts in their surroundings. I have done this largely through specific cases, looking at the situations that obtained in several universities. I have attempted to examine and describe how individuals adapted and how those adaptations may have prepared them for the future while they struggled to retain some continuity with their past. I have considered those aspects of institutions that seemed to give support or appeared to add stress to faculty and students.

The book has been written in a context of increasing upheaval, of disruption, of rage at much that may well be essential in education. Four years ago I saw a trustees' meeting dramatically interrupted by a student guerrilla theater acting out its message that the meeting of the board was precious and passé. But the actors gave no indication that they knew of the crucial educational issue under discussion at the moment of their interruption. Two years ago my consulting visit to a university was cut short when tear gas was exploded over the campus by an outraged sheriff.

In 1961, I began a research project designed to define the paths that students followed during four years at the Massachusetts Institute of Technology. The focus initially was on the salient encounters that characterized their sep-

FOREWORD

arate journeys. Several of us spent considerable time looking into and then describing the psychological, intellectual, and academic characteristics of an entire class of students as they pursued their separate paths through one institution. At first our goal was to approximate the psychological and intellectual expense and benefit to the student of this four-year journey.

I wanted to understand the complexity of a campus with its subtleties and interplay of conditional causes. And I wondered how we could assess the institution's influence on the various residents—the faculty, the students, the staff. What is the application of these insights to strategies for change in the educational process? What kind of information is relevant to decisions for the present or for a decade hence? The answers to such questions would, I hoped, indicate some of the small and large forces that shaped a specific educational environment.

What began as a circumscribed study led me in time to other problems. Is a university manageable? Can it maintain the quality of human interaction that allows for education, not gamesmanship? These and other questions have more force for me today than a decade ago. After serving as a senior administrative officer in a university, I am far more aware of the importance of distraction, of the harassment of the daily decision, matters that affect what is manageable, what education is, and the possibilities for rational change.

I originally intended to write a report on a specific research project. But I came to believe that a reasonably

FOREWORD

careful look at one or even several institutions could contribute more to an understanding of the difficulties that face the system of higher education, and I decided to address myself to a broader audience. My experience reinforced the belief that from the special case of even one university, cautious generalizations about higher education as a whole are warranted. As I examined colleges, universities, and secondary schools, I was struck repeatedly with the importance of a hidden agenda, a hidden curriculum, which determined to a great degree the way in which the various participants played the game, read the cues, adapted to their immediate educational circumstances. This book is for participants in or consumers of higher education; it is not presented as a research report explaining the specifics of methodology to a more limited audience. Concluding the writing in a year of turmoil has heightened my concern for education's survival and has strengthened my decision to write for a wider audience.

I have drawn from my experience as a psychiatrist and as a consultant to particular individuals and institutions. Some may argue that M.I.T. is so unique a school that the findings can hardly be generalized. But I think it is appropriate to take a careful and intensive look at a special case and draw inferences that can be examined in a wider context. These inferences may bear on the range of man's adaptability and on the impact of the environment on man's defense against anxiety. I have found that a hidden curriculum determines, to a significant degree, what becomes the basis for all participants' sense of worth and

FOREWORD

self-esteem. It is this hidden curriculum, more than the formal curriculum, that influences the adaptation of students and faculty. I know of no kindergarten, high school, or college that is without a hidden curriculum which bears on its students and faculty. Though each curriculum has characteristics that are special to the particular setting, the presence of these hidden curricula importantly affects the process of all education. The similarities in these hidden curricula are at least as important as the differences.

M.I.T.'s special character is both germane and timely, for society must learn to live with technology, and must prevent technology from doing violence to our environment or to the development of a humane world. The processes by which we educate our scientists and engineers affect all society. We have a major stake in the successful solution to the immediate educational dilemma facing universities that educate primarily scientists and engineers.

The names of those who have contributed time and thought and energy, who have helped to educate this author fill more than one, single-spaced, typewritten page. The length of such a list, incomplete though it is, clearly indicates the extent of my intellectual debt. Early in the research project, Professor John T. Rule was a constantly insightful intellectual companion. The initial study was made possible by the Grant Foundation, and, particularly, by Adele Morrison, executive secretary of the foundation, who saw sense and promise in our initial formulation. The

FOREWORD

Education Research Center at M.I.T., the Bing Foundation, and, more recently, the National Institute of Mental Health have all provided financial support. Throughout this period, Dr. Albert Seeler, Professor Jerrold Zacharias, and Provost Jerome Wiesner have given consistent administrative help. Those students in the M.I.T. class of 1965 who gave of their time and their thought taught me much, and their faculty further contributed to my education. Martin Trow, professor of sociology, University of California, Berkeley, who interviewed the faculty as part of the original study, is the author of Chapter III. He discusses the faculty perceptions of the stresses in their relationships with their students and he has brought considerable insight to the way distraction affects both the learning and the lives of faculty and students. His chapter is evidence of our joint concern and shared education. Dr. Merton Kahne, Professor John R. Seely, Dr. Dorothy Huntington, and Dr. Malcolm Parlett played significant parts in developing the insights and implications during the period of research. Considerable additional help came from Dr. Howard Herman, Professor Harold Isaacs, Professor Franco Modigliani, Professor Gordon Kaufman, Dr. Joseph Wheelwright, Dr. Liam Hudson, Professor A. H. Halsey, and Professor Paul Heist. Several discussions with Sir Geoffrey Vickers were especially helpful as the last chapters were written. Of the research assistants, Dr. Elaine Hockman stands out as having added to our work significantly. Hilda Silverman, Florence Berger, Carolyn MacGregor, Patricia Eden, Steven Warner, James

FOREWORD

Taylor, and Linda Cato also contributed appreciably to the outcome. Nancy Rioux gave greatly of her thoughtfulness, time, and caring to make the early and middle phase of this work come to a point where a manuscript was completed. In the final stages, special thanks are due to Gene Lichtenstein, who helped put together a manuscript that had more coherence and style, and to Ashbel Green, whose persistent prodding greatly increased the quality of the final product. Annette Anderson's devotion to detail and to a publisher's deadline was an important factor in the final outcome. She was aided by Linda Omohundro. Mary Snyder's patience has been part of the context which made the book possible.

Benson R. Snyder

Cambridge, Massachusetts
July 17, 1970

THE HIDDEN CURRICULUM

1

THE TWO CURRICULA

A senior in an outstanding suburban high school recently turned down membership in the National Honor Society. He explained his decision in a letter published in the school paper.

> I have a few reasons for this action. . . . I see [the Honor Society], in general, as merely an indication that an individual has succeeded in a system that I feel wastes human potential, blunts and distorts natural curiosities, and de-emphasizes creativity, individualism, and responsibility, in order to render him more malleable. Furthermore, Honor Society, along with current grading procedures, can be seen as a goal that redirects students into an "answer-oriented" versus a "problem-oriented" outlook on education where answers become more important than the process of learning. . . .

This student is calling attention to a difference between the messages coming from the formal goals of his teachers and their curriculum, and other, contradictory messages associated with the means that students find they must use in order to attain high grades and other academic rewards. It is not necessarily true that his teachers either meant or planned to stifle his creativity or to render him more malleable, even though this may have been the outcome of high school education for many students.

The assignments given in the classroom and the rewards for superior work are not limited to the formal curriculum. While many tasks are cast in explicit terms—"Do problems 1 through 8 on page 67," "Read Chapter 3 and be prepared to discuss the period 1792–94 in French politics"—there is another set of less obvious tasks which bears a most interesting and important relationship to the formal curriculum. The question for the student is not only what he will learn but how he will learn. These covert, inferred tasks, and the means to their mastery, are linked together in a hidden curriculum. They are rooted in the professors' assumptions and values, the students' expectations, and the social context in which both teacher and taught find themselves.

How does it happen that students, often the most able, turn off from their education? Why do honest, imaginative efforts to enrich, to open up, to alter the curriculum fail to engage so many students? In trying to answer these questions, I have repeatedly been led by my experience to the importance of the context, the emotional and social surround, of the formal curriculum. All that follows in one way or another explores the consequences of the formal

THE TWO CURRICULA

curriculum's context for education, for educational institutions, and for the individuals who live within them, for a few years as students or for decades as members of the faculty.

When students first come to a college campus as freshmen, most are disoriented. Each is busy developing a cognitive map of the campus—finding the appropriate paths to the proper places. In practical terms, students are getting a fix on the requirements—that is, on the formal curriculum. They learn quickly which course options are open to freshmen; how to drop introductory English; what specific prerequisites are needed for the first-year physics course; and how to keep a scholarship. In addition—as part of the formal curriculum—they soon become familiar with the nonacademic rules, and with the explicit sanctions for breaking them: for example, the nature of the college's stand on drugs, the penalty for coeds who fail to sign out.

During the first few days, the students move from one official class to the next, and listen to the professors outlining assignments for the term and explaining about quizzes, lab work, and term papers. By combining systematic recognizance and intuition, they come to realize that the faculty expect them to acquire certain information and to develop enough competence to work problems in physics, take tests in history, or write themes in freshman English.

In practice this is almost always translated by students

into a series of discrete, more or less manageable tasks which they infer is the actual basis for the grade their professors will give them. Three-hour exams, a ten-page paper, a reading list of four books, etc., become the tasks to be mastered for the professor's approval. Such tasks then lead students to a set of tactics or maneuvers. One student budgeted his time and commitment in a math course by doing the last problem in the nightly homework set of six. He assumed it contained all the necessary principles. Only if he had difficulty would he then do the fifth, fourth, etc. He saw the course as consisting of these "hurdles" drawn up by the professor. He said this "exercise" would prepare him well enough for the ultimate race —the examination. In the same way, students translate "understanding" physics or English literature or sociology into mastering a set of tasks which may or may not have much to do with learning, or even knowledge. On many campuses they find that only part of the assigned work needs to be completed (in some particular cases only part of the work *can* be completed—but more on this later). This is usually the student's initial experience with the dissonance between the formal curriculum and the hidden curriculum with its latent, covert tasks that students (and others) infer as the basis for the rewards in the particular setting.

The students also come to know how their deans and their advisers actually react to infringements of parietal hours, to "hacking around," or to campus protests. In effect, they are constantly asking questions about the differences between the formal and the hidden curriculum: What are the actual hurdles one must jump? How important is the style or form, or is it enough simply to get over the hurdle? What is the generally accepted academic and social behavior within the university, and how is this reflected in the formal rules and explicit prescriptions? The answers to these and many similar questions form the syllabus of the hidden curriculum. For most students, it is more important than the visible curriculum during their freshman year.

Nevertheless, the hidden curriculum is rarely talked about openly with the faculty or with deans. There is some distrust of those who set its tasks. It is, at most, a semiprivate matter, shared with roommates and certain classmates. This semiprivate nature of the hidden curriculum is essential to its existence. The more it becomes public, the more it becomes part of the formal curriculum. Some of the hesitation in discussing these tasks comes from the students' initial uncertainty about the accuracy of their perception. But there is another reason for the comparative silence about the hidden curriculum: it is related to the differences—in attitudes, norms, and perceptions—which exist among undergraduates. To one student, his professor is "wreaking his vengeance" on all of them by controlling their grades. To another, the formal classwork is an exercise in manipulation, in which the professor knows all the answers to all the questions and all the trivial

THE HIDDEN CURRICULUM

exercises laid out before the students. But a third talks about academic life as a setting where he is free to make mistakes, free to explore along with the professor any and all issues that come to mind.

In the next chapter one student, Jones, speaks of the hidden curriculum, in contrast to the high school student's comment. By figuring out its syllabus in the first few weeks of his freshman year, he was able to get the highest grade with the least expenditure of effort. Another student, Moore, spent most of his time in a thermodynamics course reading textbooks and references to the literature because he saw the formal classwork as an exercise in manipulation. The professor was seen as simply eliciting answers to questions for grading purposes; the student felt that he would not really obtain sufficient grasp of the fundamentals from doing his professor's exercises. He made his judgment of what to do on the basis of his deep interest in the field and his desire to understand it.

Midway through his freshman year another student, Brown, was told by a dean that his poor academic showing was proof that his admission had been a mistake. (He had, in fact, been termed a "high risk" by the admissions office.) Brown was discouraged by this piece of intelligence. Since he knew he was capable of hard work, he went about examining his courses to see where sustained, hard work would most likely influence his grades. He didn't share this strategy with the dean, with his professors, or even with classmates, because of the acute shame he felt at his own marginal status. He seemed afraid that his brain was simply not up to standard; as a freshman higher grades became the only way to assure himself as well as his professors of his worth.

How the student perceives these quite different class settings and professors comprises an important segment of the hidden curriculum. Each student figures out what is actually expected as opposed to what is formally required. A professor may explain at the beginning of the term that he requires knowledge and competence and creativity and originality. In many cases, the professor may mean it; or he may believe what he has said but then sets the tasks in such a way that rote memory rather than knowledge is rewarded. It takes the class a little time to sort out these messages, to locate the disparity, to interpret the mixed signals created by the presence of both a formal and a hidden curriculum. The university is not the only institution in which this kind of double system occurs. Certainly it is present within most groups and organizations—corporations, families, government. What is crucial is not the presence of formal rules and informal responses but rather the kinds of dissonance that are created by the distance between the two; and the way that employers and workers, parents and children, professors and students work out, clarify, and discuss the conflicts and issues that are often concealed.

THE HIDDEN CURRICULUM

There is no single response to this disjunction between the two curricula. Some students even fail to recognize that a disjunction exists. But nearly all of them find that they must develop a series of stratagems, of ploys and adaptive techniques, to deal with the choices that confront them.[1] They know that they must complete assignments,

[1] *Adaptive, adaptation, cope,* and related terms are used throughout this book. Obviously, it is important for the reader to understand how I define these words. As a first step, the definition of *adaptation* and *cope* in Webster's Dictionary sharpens the difference between these terms. Adaptation is defined as "modification of an animal or plant fitting it more perfectly for existence under the conditions of its environment." On the other hand, *cope* is defined as "to strike, to fight, to struggle or contend . . . with."

Adaptive mechanisms refers to those mental processes which alter the inner state of the individual so as to significantly affect the subsequent interaction with the environment. *Adaptation* is used, then, as a descriptive term referring to those intrapsychic processes which have a demonstrable effect on the quality of the individual's interaction with his environment. The changes occur primarily in the individual in response to outside stimuli.

Defense mechanisms refers to those mental processes with which the individual responds to the emergence into consciousness of instinctual strivings. A defense mechanism's primary function is to keep the emotional or the ideational representatives of these strivings out of consciousness. The changes occur within the individual in response to internal stimuli. There is some dispute between psychoanalysts as to whether defense mechanisms, in addition to containing conflict, also assist in the resolution of the conflict. Where this occurs, a defense mechanism would serve constructive ends as well.

A defense mechanism can be an adaptive mechanism in another way, depending on the vantage point of the observer. If the observer is concerned primarily with the impact of a particular mental process (such as denial, projection, reaction formation, etc.) on the individual's inner state (i.e., if the defensive function is the focus of attention), it would be called a defense mechanism. Should the observer turn his attention to the environmental consequences of that same mental process, its adaptive function will be in the foreground. For this discussion I have

write papers, pass examinations; that they must organize their time and decide between work and pleasure. In this sense the disjunction forces them to decide on priorities—whether to explore a question in great detail or to aim for a grade, if time and pressure do not permit both. It also tends to determine which choices will provide the student with the greatest sense of self-satisfaction, for it focuses on the manner in which he maintains his own self-regard: he must choose between, or link, what he expects of himself with what others, in varying degrees, expect of him. If it is honors and high grades, he feels compelled to play one kind of game—in his choice of courses and professors, the kinds of questions he raises, the research he pursues. For it is clear to him that the reward structure of the professor and the university are often closely tied to a particular kind of performance. If he seeks the avoidance of failure—a way of getting by with a minimum of difficulty—he may choose another set of ploys and prepare work only when it will be graded, "psych out" the professor's interests, avoid involvement.

---

labeled "adaptive mechanisms" those mental processes which are primarily concerned with influencing and changing the individual's relationship to his environment by means of altering the inner state.

Coping patterns I take to refer to some behavior, some action which alters the individual's relationship to his environment. A coping pattern, in order to be so named, must have some influence on the individual's adaptation to the environment by altering his behavior in relation to that environment. Clearly there is always some secondary shift in the individual's internal state as a result. The changes here occur primarily in the environment in response to internal stimuli.

THE HIDDEN CURRICULUM

The strategy differs for each student, though all develop a series of adaptive techniques in an effort to deal with the new environment and some of its more confusing characteristics. For example, most students discover within the first month of college that they cannot possibly complete all the assigned work. To finish all the tasks of the formal curriculum would require far more time than is available. In a typical coping pattern the student finds he must neglect, selectively, certain aspects of the formal curriculum. He must learn what he can avoid doing, knowing where the risks are minimal and the cost is modest. The message is unstated, but it is as clear to the student as an item of information in the college catalogue.

There is a decided value in this system for the student. He is forced to make judgments about what is relevant; he develops a method of study and fixes a way of budgeting his time. But it may also foster a sense of gamesmanship and make the encounter between the student and the professor a competitive rather than a cooperative one. Some students, for example, schedule their time to the minute; others work hard only under pressure and seem to exist from one academic crisis to another. A third group plays the academic game by ear; another turns it off altogether.

When students in an introductory course for freshmen were told that problem sets would be handed in at the beginning of each class and graded at mid-term, they first determined how much the homework would contribute to the final grade. When they discovered that, in fact, it would not count at all, they converted the information to their own ends. They continued to work occasional problems but took elaborate care to fill in the same amount of space on the homework papers as they had at the beginning of the term. They were afraid that the professor might get wise and thereafter include the homework as a factor in the final grade.

In a similar way the "dope sheets" on the faculty often exacerbate the competitive game that they are designed to beat. Does the professor like essays flavored with philosophical irony? Has he a special interpretation of T. S. Eliot's poetry? Does he insist on a particular form in working out solutions to mathematical problems? In an ironic way, the professor becomes the consumer and the student the seller of the desired goods. These informal tactics are familiar to most students; they are part of college lore. At the same time they force some undergraduates into a kind of game they are not seeking to play. Classmates and the professor have become locked into the situation, and it requires considerable discipline and strength to break out of it.

The faculty is not playing a duplicitous game, but the processes that the system has created tend to work against the ends desired by the professors, the students, and the university. It is these processes—and not malice or sadism on the part of teachers—that help perpetuate the gap between the two curricula. Not all the signals that are picked up about the professor's actual intent are, however, distorted. "Professor X is cruel—watch out for him—don't expose yourself, or he'll shaft you," explained one student. On investigation this turned out to be a fairly realistic appraisal of the behavior and educational philosophy of Professor X. The college system is such that the professor can work out his own philosophy, as well as his aggressions, on students. He can chop them down because they seem too independent, arrogant, creative; or because they are too casual, careless, condescending. Obviously only a few professors are looking to make scapegoats and victims out of their students, but many other members of the faculty seem to get caught up by the contest. A professor may inadvertently adopt the role assigned to him by students and fellow faculty members, and increasingly become a cynic, wit, detached man, or watchdog at the gate.

The fact is that, while most professors do want their students to explore ideas, generate new questions, and engage in intellectual risk-taking, they find themselves caught in a trap that militates against these goals. Large classes, rigid testing methods, overextended scholars who derive their principal rewards from research, all reinforce the system.

Thus it is not surprising that students consistently redefine the tasks of the formal curriculum set by the faculty. Learning calculus is converted into a series of discrete operations, as in the case of the student who started his homework at the end rather than the beginning of the assignments. One does only those problems that will be graded or that will appear on an examination; or, on another level, one seeks to give the appearance of industry and attentiveness, if there is any chance that this will influence the grade. Thus alienation becomes concealed behind a coat and tie or behind attendance at class. It is as much a form of alienation—perhaps an even more profound manifestation of alienation—than any student sit-in.

At the center, of course, are the grades. Not only do they certify accomplishment, but many future rewards are dependent on them—graduate school, fellowships, recommendations, career. Moreover, despite a physics professor's enthusiasm for experimentation and creativity, he may award a grade on the basis of tests alone, which in turn measure the student's ability to negotiate and play back under pressure a specified amount of required information.

In an English course an essay may be broken down into component parts by students. Style and certain facts are woven together in a fabric which the students have come to know will strike their professor's eye. The point is similar; judgments are made on minimal cues which students have figured out and presented for the grade.

Even when the student decides to court the risk, to possibly sacrifice the grade in order to pursue some intellectual problems that interest him, he often is beset by conflict. Many intellectual students find that their own self-esteem has become caught between the formal and the hidden curricula. They are scornful of the way these operate, but it has become important for them to gain the recognition that follows from an A, or, as Malcolm Parlett's study[2] suggests, to avoid the loss of self-esteem resulting from a D or an F. For some, the reward and the accompanying feeling of self-approval have replaced the excitement of learning. One student told me, "If I wanted to work at a problem and stop and think about it for a while, maybe even doing some independent work on it, there just wasn't any opportunity to do this; and I felt myself rebelling against the compartmentalized courses. There was very little thinking."[3]

I observed the professor in one class beginning the term by explaining that the students were expected to be cre-

---

[2] "Undergraduate Teaching Observed," *Nature*, Vol. 223, No. 5211 (Sept. 13, 1969), pp. 1102–4.

[3] Originally suggested by Talcott Parsons and used extensively by David Reisman and Martin Trow, the instrumental and expressive roles are useful characterizations of two frequent modes of involvement in the educational experience. The instrumental student has a pragmatic approach to education, where the validity of an action is determined by its successes, the validity of an idea by its utility. Such students ask themselves how (or whether) the study of a text or the writing of a paper can help them achieve a higher grade and thus further their specific career or life plans. These students want to know how their present behavior will further their ends. Instrumental students try to make "the best" investment of time and energy as a means to their goal. The expressive student has a more idealistic approach to education, in which the validity of an action or an idea is determined more by its impact on the individual's inner experience. The expressive student asks how he can know himself, his capacities, potentials, limitations, and then express these. Such students are concerned with communicating their thoughts, and the manner of that expression is important. Studying a text, the expressive student first considers how the text may contribute to his understanding, and only secondarily how knowledge of the text will contribute to his grade.

THE TWO CURRICULA

ative and involved; in short, they were to be engaged. They would have the opportunity to take intellectual risks, to make mistakes. When I talked with the students in the class I discovered that many were quite surprised by his introductory statement; a few were puzzled and suspicious, others enthusiastic.

Five weeks later the first quiz was given. The students found that they were asked to return a large amount of information that they could only have mastered by memorization. There was a considerable discrepancy between the students' expectations for the course and what they were in fact expected to learn in order to pass the quiz. In spite of the professor's opening pronouncements, the hidden but required task was *not* to be imaginative or creative but to play a specific, tightly circumscribed academic game.

The consequences for the students varied: some became cynical and said, "Okay, if that's the way you play the academic game, if that's what he really wants, I won't make the same mistake again. Next time I'll memorize the key points." Some students were discouraged and simply withdrew emotionally from the class, though they nominally remained in attendance and received satisfactory grades. But a large group approved the quiz. They had been apprehensive about their capacity to do original work and were relieved to find that rote memory would suffice to get a superior grade. Students of this latter group were, interestingly, the least likely to consult the college psychiatrist.

THE HIDDEN CURRICULUM

It is easy to view the existence of the hidden curriculum as an accidental design, one in which the academic process has somehow managed to thwart the real interests of the university. Professors and students, presumably, *are* interested in learning, growth, and certain intellectual excitement. But instead they find themselves unexpectedly trapped by grades (and grading), competition for success and the rewards that accompany it, and institutionalization. Everyone may profess to know better, but the self-esteem of teachers and students alike is inevitably tangled in the process; and it is difficult to cut out and ignore the grades, competition, and rewards which have become so internalized.

This view of the situation, however, ignores the fact that the academy has itself created the system and that it serves a protective function, permitting a minimum amount of risk-taking and protecting the maintenance of the educational status quo. It is not that students necessarily want to avoid academic risks; it is just that they learn early in their educational career that few rewards accompany such risks.

Nor are the professors all conservatives, committed to the maintenance of the status quo. One professor at a leading eastern university explained:

> When I first came here, there were four of us, all sharp, knowledgeable social scientists, down from Harvard, all arriving within two years of one another. We thought we'd really have a say in running the department. And

THE TWO CURRICULA

we *were* allowed a voice in departmental matters. But we were also given extraordinary freedom to go our own ways. We each sought out bright students who were interested in the same things we were and took them on as graduate students. We taught whatever courses we wanted in whatever way we chose. We were saddled with a very small amount of committee and paper work, which means that we were able to get on with our research, our writing, our contacts (which were important for both our teaching and our professional competence) outside of the university. The Provost and department chairman took all the university burdens off our back, provided us with the freedom and the protection to carry on this way. And for us it was a grand life. The only trouble was that the university apparently went down the drain right under our noses, and we never even knew it.

The hidden curriculum comes even more sharply into focus when one considers the network of rules and regulations governing the student's social conduct. For here, too, there are both formal and hidden agenda. The rules are spelled out so that the university can function in a parental role, particularly with respect to the conduct of women students. Parietal rules govern the hours when women are permitted in the men's dormitory rooms (in most schools men are not permitted in the women's dormitory rooms) and stipulate hours when women have to be in at night. The coeds are constantly enjoined to behave like ladies, which appears to mean that they have to be careful in their relationships with men. Some of this is disappearing, especially at elite colleges. But many universities still maintain close surveillance on the manners and mores of their coeds.

At one coeducational university, the handbook defined suitable behavior for coeds out on a date and proceeded to define a date as "being in the presence of a boy for fifteen minutes." Another posted a ban on coeducational sunbathing, while a large state university counted late infractions by the minute and meted out punishment by the accumulation of minutes: for every sixty seconds that a woman returned to her dormitory after hours she lost five minutes the following Saturday. If her total over the term exceeded thirty late minutes, she was confined to quarters for an entire weekend. At another state university regulations called for a couple in a men's dormitory room "to have three feet on the floor at all times."

Such explicit rules with clearly defined restrictions and punishments would seem to be straightforward enough, except that the students know the rules are designed for another, often unstated, purpose. They exist to make it as difficult as possible for students to couple on campus property. Any student foolish enough to be detected may be dismissed from the university. This has been common enough practice; although several years ago, when a coed threatened to sue a university for its action suspending her for a year (she was white and living with a boy who was black), the university backed down and reinstated her. It simply was not worth the risk of confrontation, racial antagonism, and undue publicity. Besides, she was intelligent, a high academic performer, and the professors had long resented having to fulfill the parental role. The deans who prescribe these rules are usually saying to the students: either do that sort of thing off campus, or else don't get caught.

The students, of course, were usually aware of the mixed signals and responded to them in different ways. For some they were a relief. They wanted the parental authority plus the hidden structure that allowed them to contravene it when they chose. At one college where rules were rather strictly enforced, the women were offered two informal choices. They could entertain men in small rooms off the main dormitory living room known as passion parlors; here they had the knowledge of the nearness of housemothers who were prepared to see that students avoided falling into compromising positions. Or they could use the adjacent parking lot which the college had provided. In effect, what they had was privacy in the parking lot or a certain amount of parental-type observation in the dormitory. Recently the women students challenged the college's hypocrisy. They wanted the dean to acknowledge that men could enter their rooms and spend the night as well. In asking for permission they were also seeking approval, for a consequence of the hidden curriculum is that students often distrust those adults on campus who are responsible for the rules. They were extremely cautious, generally, about discussing anything that touched on sex and restricted such conversations with the deans and most of the faculty to a minimum.

The same kind of dissonance exists in most schools over the issue of pregnancy. There tends to be no communication between student and either dean or professor when a girl becomes pregnant. Usually, with the help of a friend, she finds her way to an abortionist, for the college's response in the past has often been an angry and immediate dismissal. Thus it is little wonder that students are reluctant to discuss sex, pregnancy, dating, or the Pill with faculty members or administrators. In countless ways they feel a dramatically diminished sense of trust; they are exposed to clearly defined rules, but the real issues are left unstated.

During the past few years students have begun to challenge not only the rules but the assumptions that lie behind them. Most have won extensions of or an end to parietal hours, and coeducational dormitories are now emerging. But the basic principle in question is whether the university has the right to govern the student's private life. And if it does, on what basis does it arrive at a given set of values and behaviors? Some universities are abandoning the business of regulating the student's social conduct. Their administrators are no longer so certain that their own social codes must be followed by the students, and it is not an issue they want to contest. The dean who

THE TWO CURRICULA

sees himself as *in loco parentis* can no longer count on unequivocal faculty support.

Here is one area where sweeping changes within universities are occurring and will continue to occur. It is not certain that there will be any less distrust or any more discussions on matters of pregnancy and sex, but there may be less hypocrisy and friction. (It should be emphasized that for all of their sophistication students often have limited or inaccurate knowledge about such matters as the Pill, abortion, and the psychological consequences of having intercourse at eighteen, and would like to talk about them with someone who is knowledgeable and interested and whom they can trust.) Rather, what appears to be occurring is a political shift, or a transfer of power from university administrators to students, with the latter sharing the major responsibility for determining rules and social conduct. By comparison, it will be a great deal more difficult to induce faculty members to share with students the making of decisions over curriculum matters, for faculty members are not nearly as ambivalent as the deans about their hidden curriculum and are much less willing to transfer power to the students.

The shifts in power do not necessarily mean that learning has been advanced very far, or that discussion has begun between students and teachers or deans on issues of some moment in the immediate (and future) lives of the undergraduates, or that there is any more trust or communication. Nor does it mean that the students themselves will not provide their own hidden agenda or their own form of hypocrisy. In place of university sanctions, they may well substitute the pressures of their own culture on those who falter or resist conforming to their norms. It is precisely for this reason that some students seek the rules and standards that the university provides. They are too unsure of their own judgment and too easily intimidated by their classmates.

For it is clear that, in addition to pressures and rules laid down by professors and deans, students have their own peers to contend with. They interact with one another, take on new roles, adopt new sets of norms, and adjust to the student culture. Most of the pressure relates to the student's private life—drugs, sexual mores, social attitudes, and perhaps most important of all, the way in which things are done.

The freshman discovers that many distinctions between groups of students are being drawn by classmates (and professors as well)—distinctions that are alluded to in a glance, a smile, or a word. These may well determine where a student will live and who his friends will be. If he is perceptive and keeps his eyes and ears open, he will find that these groups differ in their shared view of the world, in the moral or ethical position they take toward cheating in the classroom or sex in the bedroom. The only outward sign of these differences may be the way the students dress or wear their hair.

Thus the central task of the hidden curriculum for the

THE TWO CURRICULA

student is to learn which patterns of behavior are tribally and/or institutionally sanctioned. He must come to know the social and psychological effect on his friends (as well as the faculty) of the cut of his clothes, the length of his hair, the tone of his voice, his choice of posters and records, the quality of his academic performance. He must understand the difference that it makes on campus whether he carries a brief case or a green bag, whether he gets straight A's or casual C's. The details may seem trivial, but the pressure for him to conform, to adjust to a particular social and psychological climate established by his peers, is a profound one. The difference between this and the formal rules spelled out in the catalogue is that the student has the relative freedom to choose among alternative subcultures, much as he might choose among competing fraternities. But the students themselves can be as sadistic and demanding as the most tyrannical professor. And the problem for each student is how to manage or cope with this covert student culture which represents such an important section of the hidden curriculum.

One student boasted about the erotic happenings that took place in his room each Sunday afternoon. Later he explained that he really spent the afternoons with his date listening to the New York Philharmonic in his room while she brewed tea and sewed curtains for his windows. The last thing he could acknowledge to his friends was the tenderness and relatively uncomplicated intimacy which they had experienced together. Everyone expected sexual play and raised no further questions, and he avoided ridicule.

The style of a different set would make it unthinkable for the student to talk about his sexual activities and his girl friend. Instead, he might make it clear that she was "a good scout," or that their day had been spent drinking beer or smoking pot, that they were somehow comrades with a certain amount of sex thrown in. This style is perhaps much more influenced by prep or high school norms, and is another way of disavowing intimacy and tenderness. The university has no difficulty approving one aspect of the domestic scene, namely listening to music together, drinking tea (even when a hot plate is forbidden in the student's room), and sewing curtains; but its officials may respond punitively when the erotic side is displayed. Both faculty and students may be against the rules, and infractions of some of the rules may be overlooked, but the erotic behavior is punished.

How does all this affect the hidden curriculum? For one thing, it tells students, particularly women, that they must gain their sexual experience by learning how to be discreet, by becoming adept at playing a game of deceit. Given the formal rules and the reality of the hidden curriculum, this is the strategy that pays off. Further, it means that very often the students who come to the attention of a dean and are referred to a counselor or psychiatrist for some "sexual misdemeanor" are those who either are naïve or want to be caught and punished.

The much more fundamental and more human issue of intimacy is often shortchanged or ignored; and, far more serious for the student's later development, such intimacy becomes associated with shame. At the other extreme, in some institutions many students feel that they cannot acknowledge openly that they do not know the dose of the Pill or the name of an obstetrician who can diagnose pregnancy. The pressure on them from students is to avoid any such admission, to be sophisticated, not to be frank or open about ignorance on such matters.

There is a tendency for many educators to dismiss the student subculture as simply an expression of youth's style. They not only deny the critical presence of two curricula but also the connection between the classroom and the dormitory. The consequences of this kind of perception for both the student and the university are severe. The student's method of coping and his form of adaptation extend far beyond the classroom, beyond even his life in the dormitory. What happens during his exposure is not isolated from, nor independent of, his style of dealing with them two or four or eight years later. These events, as with all encounters in the college, become part of the educational process which shapes the student's later life. If one treats the two curricula as separate, with little or no influence on each other, if one ignores the efforts of students to manage them simultaneously (just as they attempt to respond to the pressures from faculty and from peers, as they try to make social and academic distinctions and judgments), a very simple, trivial model of education may emerge; motivation becomes equated with "not being lazy," learning with conformity to formal, required tasks. When the principles embodied in this simplified model become the basis for faculty decisions about the educational process itself, about changes and reform in the selection, grading, or disciplining of students, the result is usually an inadvertent increase in the educational conflicts between students and faculty. One difficulty is that professors are more obtuse collectively than individually about these matters. Another is that professors, as a rule, have tended in the past to view such matters as intrusions. Now that they are challenged by students who often seem to them arrogant, ill-informed, and anti-intellectual, they are quite easily capable of dismissing the real issue of the two curricula under the guise of dealing with "political" students. The educator who self-righteously persists in this attitude will almost certainly forfeit the chance to listen to students and thus to learn from them. And the student who maintains an antagonistic attitude toward professors will suffer a similar loss. The perilous consequences, for students, faculty, university—indeed, for society—are readily evident.

2

SELECTIVE NEGLIGENCE, COMPETENCE, AND COMMITMENT

> *I think the most important task is to keep plugging away. . . . Some days I'm riding high, and the next day I'm just down in the dumps. It doesn't matter what I was doing, trying to get a date and get shot down, maybe do poorly on an exam. The person who is always plugging away, never gives up, usually comes through in the end.*
> *The pressure is always there, subtly: How well are you doing this term? . . . I don't know exactly where the pressure comes from. Whether it's pride or ego or a fear that if you don't get the straight A you won't go to grad school or you won't get the fellowship. I don't know.*

This student was one of the fifty-four who participated in a study of student adaptation[1] that began in 1961. I had become particularly interested in the unintended,

[1] Supported by the Grant Foundation from 1961–6, the Bing Foundation in 1967, and subsequently by the National Institute of Mental Health (present grant No. 5 R12 MH16347–03 SRC).

latent stresses which appeared to influence what students felt and how they learned. These stresses also affected the choices that they made as they moved along their individual paths through the Massachusetts Institute of Technology.[2] The students spoke at length about the reward structure which they found in college. Most of them discussed the effects it had on their developing academic competence and how it influenced the judgments they made about their worth as students. For a number, their worth as students became linked to their judgment about their worth as human beings. The students (and in a related part of the study, the faculty) spoke of strains in their encounters. These strains developed in response to stresses located in the social structure of the university—stresses located in the hidden curriculum.

Five students in this chapter reflect the range of responses. Their own voices are placed in the context of their lives at the time they spoke with me. Much detail has been omitted. My object here is to give a sense of

[2] In addition to a larger study of the entire nine hundred members of the class of 1965, a random, stratified sample of that class was interviewed four times, for those who remained during their four years. These interviews were all taperecorded and transcribed. The students' interviews were evaluated independently by Drs. Merton Kahne and Dorothy Huntington, consultants to the project.

B. Snyder; 1967; Report on Student Adaptation Study, Education Research Center, M.I.T., Cambridge, Mass.

E. Hockman, M. Kahne, M. Parlett; 1967; Omnibus Personality Inventory; Appraisal of Findings; Education Research Center, M.I.T., Cambridge, Mass.

NEGLIGENCE, COMPETENCE, COMMITMENT

how the students felt, how they learned and made choices during their time in school.

As a nineteen-year-old sophomore, Moore had just begun to major in the science field in which he subsequently received his Ph.D. He spoke about his experience and that of his classmates with vivid imagery. For example, he described M.I.T. laughingly as the huge beast. The instructor was "wreaking his vengeance" on one of his classmates with a low grade. This imagery, however, was embedded in a coherent account, which he presented with a humorous, slightly ironic twist, as he described the scene around him. He did not see most professors as deliberately sadistic; rather, the competitive social structure at times seemed to him to cast them in such a role.

Moore, who consistently made A's, had much to say about grades. His discussion illustrates a major stress in the hidden curriculum which affected the way his classmates learned and the way they felt about themselves. His high grades were not alone responsible for his relative objectivity about these stresses.

> They provide the motivation with things like grades here, but grades become a sub-goal. People come to a place like this for knowledge. It is very difficult to work toward something as intangible as knowledge. You do not know whether you are succeeding. When you are

through the four years, I guess you have the knowledge. You may not know how you got it, but the system has worked to that extent. It takes this kind of motivation to give you the feeling that you are succeeding.

Moore went on to describe how his classmates were intimidated by their quizzes and exams. He did well enough to feel safe himself but said he was "quietly troubled by seeing my buddies shot down by some ridiculous mistake." These students, he observed, quickly turned off their curiosity and wonder, a consequence that was not intended by the faculty. He then reflected that "the person who has the most ability will get the least out of the situation [i.e., competition for grades]. The person who has the ability may use this to get away with something, just learning it in one night." Moore was troubled by seeing classmates, especially the most able, approaching their courses like an exercise in game theory and getting rewarded for so doing. He explicitly described this situation as a major source of "dissonance" for students.

In his senior year Moore looked back over his attitudes toward grades and speculated on their effect on him.

> It may have been just a little bit of sour-grapes feeling. I was a little bitter about one course because the professor was not appreciating me at the time. He gave me a poor grade—a C—in a term paper. There is nothing like a little bit of success to take away some of the tendency toward criticizing. I can actually view things

with a little more perspective when I am succeeding than if I have to rationalize, lower my cognitive dissonance. So looking back, part of it was the problem of succeeding in these subjects. [His semester grades were high— mostly A's and only occasional B's.] And part was a genuine uncertainty about what career I wanted to go into.

He seriously considered changing his major in the field in which he has since received his doctorate. In part this was because of the dissonance between the field as he saw it then and the courses he was taking in that field, which he felt oversimplified problems and rewarded conformity.

He said it was important for him to see tangible results from his work, apart from his grades, because such feedback helped to free him from an over-reliance on the grade. This was brought out clearly as he talked with warmth about an ungraded pass/fail seminar he had taken in his freshman year. "I got as much or more out of it than anything else I have ever taken." It turned out that what he got was a feeling and an attitude about research. He had become aware that even the tedium involved in getting "some little device to work lead to new data that then shed some new light on the problem." He said that he had developed "a feel" for the physical phenomena under study. The tedium had been an integral part of his coming to see the phenomena differently. His professor had been deeply interested in the problem, and at no time did Moore see him as "putting on a demonstration. The prof was letting us in on it." Moore said he had been "permitted" to make mistakes. "I was clumsy in my own way and pleased when I could make things work." He felt he was deeply involved in his education during this seminar, "not just a victim." He used the local imagery of the hidden curriculum, the latent expectation in this seminar of not being fulfilled, of being exploited.

As a senior, Moore said:

> A major factor contributing to the success or failure of a subject is the morale of the students in the subject. Professors can do the best lecturing in the world, yet if somehow for some ridiculous little reason the morale of the students falls apart it is just all over. One of the reasons is the fact that students have to worry about their grades. We are constantly being kidded by some professors. They'll announce a quiz with the idea that "Well, you're really only worried about the grade in this subject," and we have to somehow put up with all this kidding. Yet it is put upon us. The pressure is put upon us to come up with grades.

Yet it is no one man, no faculty committee, that pressures students. There are assumptions embedded in the two curricula about how students study and how they learn. Moore came from a small town in Ohio, the oldest son of parents who had moved there from France because of World War II. He described his family as upper middle class more by their values than their income (under $12,000 a year). He saw his home life as stimulating. Both of his parents had a wide range of interests, from art and politics to mathematics and sports. Both parents worked, and worked hard, and both felt that "helping people was very important." He described his parents as people of great resourcefulness, and admired them, yet he could say with ease that he disliked some things about them. He did not feel that he was "a great distance from them," though as an M.I.T. junior he had commented that there was little that he was doing academically which he could share with them. They simply didn't understand his field. He saw this widening gulf between them as inevitable, but it saddened him somewhat.

Moore had graduated first in a high school class of 280. His mathematics and verbal SAT scores were both over 750, and his achievement scores were over 800. During high school he had put his energies into the technical side of school activities, though he also participated in some sports and played the cello in the school orchestra. He emphasized his activities with people rather than his academic achievements. He felt that his intellectual ability might have set him apart from his classmates. "It's hard to get good marks in high school and have a reputation that is very favorable with people who don't know you.

I had a lot to overcome with all the kids I didn't know well." He began dating in his junior year of high school, earlier than many of his M.I.T. classmates.

As a high school freshman he had planned to become an engineer in industry. He linked his interest in science to his ability in mathematics. The advanced and special courses he had taken in high school and at a National Science Foundation–sponsored summer program had been easy for him. He chose M.I.T. over a midwestern university because he felt it had the edge in science.

As Moore moved through his four undergraduate years, he relied less and less on grades to motivate him. He came to base his sense of worth as a student and as an individual on his ability to examine the physical and mathematical assumptions in his field. He was an articulate observer of the hidden curriculum (he called it "cognitive dissonance"), particularly where he felt that its syllabus constrained him or blocked his classmates' education. He became increasingly free of the hidden curriculum because he had many other bases for judging his worth and his competence than the reward system then in effect. Specifically, he received far more gratification from using his mind to master problems in his field than from working the assigned problem sets for the weekly recitation sections. These latter, in fact, he often left undone. He developed considerable perspective on the "Mickey Mouse" of the academic game, though even as a senior he thought it was useful for some students if not for himself.

NEGLIGENCE, COMPETENCE, COMMITMENT

Jones faced a similar set of encounters but responded quite differently. He was a very able student majoring in an engineering course. At the end of his sophomore year, he noted that grades were the result of hard work but that one should achieve them without becoming a "grind." Jones saw the hidden curriculum and its tasks as clearly as Moore and, like Moore, made straight A's. The high grade-point average appeared to be very nearly the most important basis of his sense of worth as an individual. He appeared to become increasingly instrumental in his approach to M.I.T.

By making sure that all his work was done beforehand, Jones was able to protect himself from failure—"so nothing can creep up on me." He found he could concentrate and apply his energy with a singular effectiveness. "It is dangerous if you start off a course too low"—not, it developed, because of intellectual difficulty but because he found that he might get discouraged. His response to this particular stress was to break down the various tasks of the curricula into their component parts and doubly prepare himself in the narrow terms of homework assignments. There was almost no indication that he had any of Moore's detachment or sense of irony. The hidden curriculum thus became the game to master.

Jones's only academic difficulties, which were minor, occurred in a freshman humanities subject and during his junior year in a relatively unstructured experimental engineering subject. He had two explanations: the humanities subjects were more personal than science courses; and it was difficult to know immediately what answers the professors considered correct in either the humanities or the engineering courses. Jones did not appear to be shaken by the pressures of his environment. He became increasingly adept at calculating the odds on the academic strategy that would pay off with a high grade and thus was very well informed about the major tasks of the hidden curriculum, particularly selective negligence and dedication to purposefulness.

Well into his last semester before graduation, Jones said, "Things are going good. I mean, I have no trouble with grades or anything. I still have an A+ average, so that's going fine there. I got into several grad schools and also got three scholarships." Like many of his classmates, he saw grades in terms of what they would buy and the degree as a certificate.

Later in the same interview, Jones began to elaborate on what was required to get some of those A's.

> You get some of these guys. They come up with this equation and it's beautiful by itself. It is a work of art and I don't really like it, maybe because I've got a practical orientation. This theory gets too much. They've got some classes that last two hours where you just write equations the whole time. You're like a monk; you sit in a classroom and copy everything down the guy says because you know it's going to be on the test. You take

NEGLIGENCE, COMPETENCE, COMMITMENT

out the equations and plug in numbers. Any jerk can do that. I think some other courses are much more interesting. All these things are so technical that it really frightens me, and I have no reason to be frightened of them. Not because I'm afraid I'll go into a course and I'll flunk the thing. That's obviously not true. It's never happened to me before; and I don't think it would happen to me if I went in there. But, it's just that I'm not interested; it just chases me away. I don't like to go into a class and act like a super-sophisticated dictating machine [even though in some respects this is what he in fact became]. You know, just copy it all down and spit it right back at the guy. In some other courses there isn't any of this stuff.

So as a senior he began to feel the pinch, to question. He went on to describe several subjects in management.

You know, you can't get anywhere unless you know how to deal with people, and I think this is the reason why I like the subject. They're tools, you might say, and I think that's—well, isn't that the reason for education? To pick up what you think you need in order to make something out of yourself, rather than having it forced down your throat?

In the end, it seemed, the instrumental approach prevailed. The reward system had allowed or encouraged him to define his worth as a student in rather narrow terms. His success came from mastery of the hidden curriculum,

THE HIDDEN CURRICULUM

not from an expressive involvement with his education.

Jones certainly did not like being wrong or being outdistanced in the classroom, in sports, or in activities. In his sophomore year, for example, he gave up one sport because he was physically behind his classmates and took up another where "everyone had the same equipment." He had an extraordinary need to know, to master, to get ahead by anticipating and then controlling his immediate environment. This was how he avoided failure. His personal life style had prepared him well for learning the facts necessary to handle the hidden curriculum. He did not date at M.I.T., since "women might tie you down on weekends when you have to study." He felt he could wait. He was able to adhere to his rigid schedule.

Introspective thinking did not appear to be usual for Jones; rather, he was fascinated, and had been from early adolescence, with space and distance. He pushed problems and emotions away from himself and was constantly figuring out how the institution would react, how his friends would react, how a professor would react; not how he himself felt, how he found himself reacting. It appeared that distance and space between people was "safe" to him, though it was not possible to say whether he associated closeness with friction and fighting (an interesting and relevant question for a psychoanalyst).

What was the hidden curriculum's effect on Jones? In his sixth term he was still problem-oriented, concerned with what was necessary to get ahead. His self-esteem continued to be primarily based on mastery and control of the curricula. The institution challenged him in his third year, when it put him more on his own in several unstructured courses. Working out a schedule and living by it was no longer in itself sufficient motivation. He spoke at the time of being shaken by the fear that he had lost his inner system of order and control. The fear was temporary. By his senior year the old control had returned, and he looked back with annoyance at the less structured, more open-ended assignment of the previous semester. It was at this point that he had begun to question his plans for graduate school, though he subsequently did go on and receive an advanced degree with honors.

In his courses, and in the rest of his life at school, Jones pushed as hard as he could to get as far as he could but constantly took the minimum of chances. In his studies he took known risks where he could carefully calculate his odds. As a sophomore he had spoken of picking little puddles where he could be the big frog. He had done this consistently and with considerable success. Grades for this student provided him with a fix on his position in the navigational sense. Without them, he felt lost. He may be a twentieth-century Icarus, rationalizing the means to his aspirations, not working through any alteration or re-evaluation of his aims.

If Smith had not been part of the random sample of students interviewed, we would have known almost nothing about the reasons for his academic failure. Smith had come to M.I.T. with high promise but with serious unresolved problems from his past. He was academically disqualified at the end of the second year, having failed almost all of his subjects. In spite of urgings during the research interview, Smith did not turn to any of the available helping resources, so that our only glimpse into the reasons for his difficulty came from the research interview itself. The failures posed by Smith at M.I.T. are present in anywhere from 1 to 10 percent of the students in any college.

Smith had done well in high school without the expenditure of much effort. At M.I.T. he had his very first experience of failing quizzes or not understanding almost immediately and easily all that went on in his classes. He spoke of going into an exam during his freshman year and observing the fright on the faces of his classmates. He was surprised when after half an hour he himself froze, his memory failed, and he flunked the test. He explained his almost total failure as simply a loss of memory and reacted by literally putting his books under his pillow at night with the thought that the knowledge in the books would, by osmosis, get into his head. I inferred that he was trying to use his M.I.T. education as a form of magic to strengthen his mind. All the while, he had to deal with the obvious antimagical bias in the content of his courses. He found no confirmation for his belief that the M.I.T. education could magically make him a superstudent.

NEGLIGENCE, COMPETENCE, COMMITMENT

Smith's first experience of failing a quiz occurred six weeks into his freshman year, a not uncommon event. He could not understand what was going on in his classes, became frightened, and then desperately tried to deny his fear. Passing examinations with high grades had been an indication to him that he had "special intellectual powers" that were unbeatable. The sudden experience of failure threatened this self-conception. His sense of worth as an individual appeared to have relied to a considerable degree on such reassurances as high grades in high school. The sudden drop in grades undermined his self-esteem. As the semester wore on, he finally resorted to "magical" means (the book under the pillow) to achieve the crucial A and the associated reassurance that he hoped it would give him. Since his major defense against the anxiety of defeat and failure was avoidance, Smith could not acknowledge to himself that he was anxious or scared, or even that he had failed a quiz. Avoidance and denial were penalized in this environment.

From his brief account of his childhood it appeared that in his earlier years he had believed he could not influence his parents' relationship to him. This was exemplified in his description of his father, which bordered on that of superman who could only be influenced by magic. Further, there were a number of indications that the family ethos allowed only for success and did not permit of failure or personal distress. He referred, for example, to a particular family crisis which his father had at first denied and had then explained by referring to magical and fateful forces.

During early adolescence Smith had been involved in weight-lifting and a number of contact sports. In high school the emphasis on physical strength apparently had rather suddenly been replaced by a very considerable concern with developing a potent and unbeatable intellect. Behind this emphasis on strength, both physical and intellectual, there appeared to be considerable anxiety about weakness, defeat, and possible impotence.

Science and engineering served as Smith's bridge to his defensive brand of masculinity. His encounter with M.I.T. had taken on some of the qualities of a magical initiation rite. This young man had considerable latent ability, but in technical terms his cognitive processes were caught in a pervasive neurotic bind. Thinking, learning, grade-getting, all assumed a special defensive significance which appeared to cripple his ability to see, let alone master, the tasks. He had to manipulate his environment, and in his desperate effort to maintain his self-esteem he relied on magic. A central task of the hidden curriculum in the first year, reducing the environment into comprehensible parameters, placed too great a burden on his defensive stance. During his sophomore year he became academically disqualified.

No manipulation of the environment could have brought the university into line with this student's demands or expectations. Smith's account illustrates the degree to which an individual can insulate himself from external influence. The university became a stage for acting out his inner conflicts. Smith's experience helped to pose the question for me of how a university can gain knowledge of the effects of its environment on the inner world of its students (not in order to expose the individual, to manipulate, but to learn about its impact). For example, the curriculum, the living arrangements, the grading practices all determined the extent to which specific adaptive patterns were utilized by Smith. Efforts to involve this student in a new educational experience by changing the curriculum, living arrangements, and grading practice would have been consistently unsuccessful, since he was so bound to his neurotic position that he would have been unable to respond to any of these changes sufficiently to affect his perception of the tasks.

Only a relatively few students have problems as extreme as this, but many have passed through a period in which they respond in such a manner. However, Smith's case does not explain the bulk of withdrawals from college. Most are not caught up in such extreme distortion or such severe neurotic restriction in their adaptive choices.

When Brown came to M.I.T. from the Middle West, he saw himself and was seen by the school as among the lower-ranking students of his class. By his junior year he was getting all A's, and he later finished two advanced degrees simultaneously at another excellent graduate school. In December of his sophomore year, Brown said:

> I was ready for a fight; in fact, on the results of my College Board scores, I didn't think I was going to get admitted. I was sort of expecting to flunk out. Well, I came with fire in my eyes, I guess you might say.

The achievement of good grades became a crucial hurdle for Brown—linked, for a relatively brief period, to the judgment of his worth as a student, but not to his judgment of his worth as an individual. Early in his second year he spoke of the constraint which he felt from both curricula.

> I channel all my efforts into getting good grades, and there are lots of times when you come up against something which—you'd just like to go deeper into, and this is somewhat frustrating because you can't. You just can't afford the time if you're like me. Now there are some students who don't give a damn about grades. I don't think this hurts them at all. It's probably good if you're interested in something, to go in and dig it and do some more work in it.

He described a very typical pattern of response to the selective-negligence task of the hidden curriculum.

NEGLIGENCE, COMPETENCE, COMMITMENT

Most of the time I found that I was doing all the work [for three subjects] in chunks. You'd do nothing [in a subject] for two weeks, and then you'd do three weeks' work, and then you'd usually lay off for another three weeks and then do it again. This was just because of the nature of the course. The quizzes were so easy and the material wasn't that hard, as long as they weren't going to make you prove things.

It is worthwhile to quote his response to an average grade in one of his humanities courses during this period.

I put a lot of time into the course and I really liked it, but I got a C. I suspect maybe I wasn't original enough in my answers in the quizzes, or maybe they were original and were the wrong ones. Seriously, I liked the course and I don't know why I got the C; I mean, I worked and I thought I understood a lot of it. But I didn't quite cut the mustard in the test.

He went on to describe a period of discouragement with his grades which he handled by some emotional de-investment in them while he continued to plug away.

By his junior interview he had introduced another theme as he remarked about his now being on the dean's list—"Grades are not for imagination." He knew he had come with College Board scores 100 points below his classmates' average scores. He worked hard to get "up there" to A's.

> At least I was up there. If I wanted to go to grad school or something, I wouldn't have any problem. And now it's more important to start learning some things. . . . I don't think the grades are that good a marker for intelligence. So many people seem to come up with more profound ideas than I. I don't think I'm imaginative at all. You don't have to be very imaginative to fit into the scheme of getting good grades. I'm quick and I can manipulate things fast sometimes.

He did not believe he was being rewarded for imagination. Subsequent events have demonstrated that he has this quality in very high measure. The system, however, was apparently not tapping it, as least in his view.

> I think there's a lot of luck involved . . . in good grades. Exams are good and make you study and make you try and learn the material, but whether the exams themselves are a good indication of how I understand the stuff . . . I don't know. . . . A lot of times you can rely on intuition and just hit a few high points, and they show up on the test—and there you are.

Brown's remarks about intuition indicate a central problem for higher education generally. Such intuitive judgments are indeed valuable. But does the present system and reward structure encourage them, or are they a by-product of the hidden curriculum? This certainly raises the question whether the best way to encourage intuitive judgments is as a by-product. Brown goes on:

> I can usually pick up the central theme on things that are pat, such as the introductory engineering course. Here you're not concerned with reality, and that's mainly manipulation. I didn't have any trouble with that at all.

He saw the hidden curriculum rewarding him for his skill at manipulation and not acknowledging formally the usefulness of intuition. In the hidden curriculum, high grades were often perceived as a function of manipulation, even though imagination and intuition were also involved in the process.

> I've had some brilliant professors, but you sort of have to weave all around to know what's coming off in a course, to ask questions, to know where you're hurting. . . . At times a good instructor will come into class and say, "Are there any questions?" . . . If nobody has any questions he'll say, "O.K., take out your papers and we'll give you a five-minute quiz" . . . and put you back in your place. And you just don't get feedback from that.

As a senior, Brown spoke again of the conflicting pressures generated in his several subjects for his time and attention.

THE HIDDEN CURRICULUM

> I just don't bother doing the homework now. I approach the courses so I can get an A in the easiest manner, and it's amazing how little work you can do if you really don't like the course. This just isn't the right way to approach education, particularly when you're a senior.

Even before his senior year, Brown had mastered a major aspect of the hidden curriculum: selective negligence. Specifically, he could pick out the central themes of a course, make relevant simplifications of complex, at times even contradictory, data or experience, and have the simplifications work—for example, in concrete terms of passing a quiz.

> I quickly discovered that the way to do well in the quizzes was always to ask the question, How can I approach this problem in the simplest possible manner? Because there were things that, if you had to solve them exactly, were impossible. Especially in the second term, it involved just intuiting the way the instructor would think that you should think on the exams. In fact, there may be many ways to get a correct answer, and some would be more elegant than others; but usually the simple-minded approach was the one that worked—and that's the way I did it.

Later on in the same interview, Brown generalized to a major educational problem:

NEGLIGENCE, COMPETENCE, COMMITMENT

Perhaps we're not teaching in the most efficient manner. These central ideas can be presented much more concisely; the problems could be somehow presented in a much more concise manner and leave more time for original work on the part of students.

Intuiting the professor's intent was, for Brown, in the service of gaining some time for himself to pursue his own academic interests.

. . . but the system almost makes you feel guiltiest for doing something that you'd like to do that's not required in class and that maybe you don't get a grade in. Their [his classmates' and his professors'] first assumption is that you shouldn't be wasting time on things that are outside of the class. . . . As time goes on I feel less and less guilty about these things, but I have a lot of friends who feel really guilty. You're afraid you're not going to get the A in the course, and if you're really high up there, I guess it makes a difference whether you get an A or the B or the C.

The pace, the institutionalized metronome, takes its toll. Brown's reaction is both subtle and to the point.

If you go along with the system and do all your homework on time and go to all your classes, keep up with everything at one time, and get everything done when it's supposed to be, you can stay up, but the minute you let one little thing slide, it kind of snowballs. It's amazing how very little stability there is about this plane. You're up high or you're way down here. You're fighting, you know, to get wind all the time, and maybe this contributes a little bit to [students playing the system]. . . . If you keep your nose to the grindstone, you can do it and you can stay up there. There is some satisfaction in doing it because in fact you do well in your quizzes and you feel you're smarter than the other guy.

I mean it's nice to go through with straight A's and, sure, people look at your record. Yet I know inwardly this really isn't the thing that counts. I'm not that much smarter than the other guys in my class. Maybe I saw some tricks. I know an awful lot of people who go through with straight A's that are awfully dull people, that haven't really learned what's in the courses or how to approach things. You get a lot of satisfaction out of seeing your name on the dean's list.

I've, of course facetiously, talked about beating the game, and yet I think in one way you can't underestimate that beating the clock aspect is a valid educational experience. You know, the ability to quickly run through a whole mess of facts and pick out the important thing. I think we might be able to achieve the same sort of thing in much less time. In other words, the whole process could be more efficient toward the same end and allow us more creative aspects.

Robertson knew how to study and had a mastery of his subjects which was not seriously threatened when he,

NEGLIGENCE, COMPETENCE, COMMITMENT

like Brown, did poorly on his early quizzes. He simply worked harder. This was his familiar pattern. His Fundamentalist religious faith shielded him from the questions that were raised in his classes and in bull sessions. During his first two years, he was "sold" on science and engineering.

> I usually did all the assignments in high school, not that I had to do them, but there was nothing else to do. I might as well do them, and you would probably learn something.

Shortly after the Christmas break of sophomore year, Robertson began to feel depressed; simply working harder did not "pay off. I just want to have time to stop, forget about the work and about the technical world for a while." He wondered during this period whether he was "missing something" and described his education as "more or less a battlefield."

> I admit life is going to be a battle all the way through. You have got to fight for what you want, and you will get your medals of honor when you are through here. You have got your proof. I went through it. I was able to fight and I raked my brain to the bone, but you might have seen your best buddy shot to pieces.

He felt pressured from having too much to do, with insufficient time to do it. The academic demands on his time were great, edging out participation in sports or pushing them to the periphery, and this competition for time accentuated the choices that he had to make. Especially, he felt encroachment on his religious life, and at the same time began to question seriously many of his religious assumptions. He described the period as very painful.

During an interview in his junior year, he looked back to his discouraged sophomore period. "I was sort of shook up. . . . I had never been so exposed before. School was replacing what I thought was most important instead of supplementing it." Education, he remarked, should not be at the expense of his religious faith.

He fought out the crises of his belief within himself during the summer between his sophomore and junior years. His family had told him he was "unlivable" without quite knowing why. But by the time he returned for his junior year he had decided:

> I could live with what I have been taught. It's back on the same level that it was in high school. Some things cannot be explained any way else but by faith. I'm just sort of willing to accept it that way.

The certain, unambiguous, and relatively noncompetitive world that he had lived in prior to M.I.T. was threatened for a time by the questions and the pressures of his first two years. His sophomore grades dropped as he questioned his commitment to science.

NEGLIGENCE, COMPETENCE, COMMITMENT

My plans were, when I graduate, to go to grad school, get a Ph.D. You know, when you are small, you think, "When I grow up, I am going to become a famous scientist and I am going to discover something and help humanity."

When he examined his life goals at the age of nineteen, in the context of all that had happened in his sophomore year (academically, socially, and psychologically), he felt strongly that he wanted to "really do something where I could help someone else." He could not see himself achieving this as "just another guy in a line in a lab for a big company." He was also afraid that he might become so "completely wrapped up in biology that I wouldn't even notice if the President of the U.S. were standing next to me."

"I have moved on to something I really didn't come here for in the first place." Instead of science, he began to see himself having a career in elected public service, a public administrator, in time, at a policy level. "School has become much more meaningful, and I feel more like working this year than I did last year, but when the time comes I say quit." Robertson had learned to neglect selectively and had put a boundary around the institution's demands on his time.

Though he continued in biology, he was clear that "one of the only concrete ideas after three years is, I do not want to go into science." His grades in all subjects, however, went up, and by his senior year he reported enjoying his senior thesis "immensely." This was in part because of "a really fantastic professor. . . . He has been really helpful as far as anything I need—equipment, advice, help. He is very successful."

Both of Robertson's parents had had limited education beyond high school and had brought up their family of one son and one daughter in a middle-class suburb. Their son characterized it as "a nice, quiet place where nothing happens, absolutely nothing." He saw his parents as strict in discipline and firm in their religious convictions. There was no tradition of higher education in his extended family. His family had not, as far as he could say, made any efforts to push him to go to college. They would be disappointed, but understanding, if he did not graduate from M.I.T.

On the basis of two interviews in his sophomore year, we inferred that his environment prior to M.I.T. had been somewhat constricted and his horizons had appeared to be bounded by a literal, almost concrete view of man. During the first few interviews, he expressed only slight curiosity about the world outside of his current academic pursuits. He appeared to be primarily interested in controlling his environment, manipulating its elements to maintain an island that was free of the dissonance and competition that surrounded him. As a scientist, he would contribute to humanity; M.I.T. was his means to this end.

NEGLIGENCE, COMPETENCE, COMMITMENT

Robertson thought the university rewarded him for doing a "huge" amount of work in a limited time, and he came to fear that these demands would ultimately encroach upon his previous basis for judging his worth—that is, having a caring relationship with his friends and leading a religiously meaningful life. In addition to these time demands, the content of his courses challenged his earlier system of values and further jeopardized the basis for his self-esteem. The scientific ethos was beginning to get under his skin.

The institution was asking him to question his beliefs and to compete against his peers. Since his pattern of behavior was to compromise in interpersonal relations, to take care of those who were less fortunate than he, the necessity for becoming a "ruthless" competitor posed a special threat to his own image of a "good person." Robertson had grown up in a family who allowed him neither to compete nor to acknowledge his anger at being "slapped down." He moved into an educational environment where he perceived "slapping down" as an everyday event. This rekindled the anxiety against which he appeared to have defended himself in his childhood adjustment by being a "good boy" on his mother's terms, never asking questions, isolating his anger and not expressing it. These same elements were present in his response to competition in the university.

He reacted to these pressures by moving across the

Charles River to a fraternity house. The Massachusetts Avenue bridge became his "drawbridge." Safely across the river, he withdrew somewhat from the competition and put his energy into helping freshmen in his living group learn the ropes. He avoided a growing sense of hopelessness in the winter of his sophomore year by shifting his relevant world from his academic major to being helpful to the freshmen. As a senior he recalled his anger rather than the pain that had characterized this period. He had completed his private retreat from science by his junior year. "I'll keep the same aims, but maybe I won't achieve them through science." His formal major remained unchanged.

Most adolescents examine and re-evaluate their ideals and life goals and, as a result, shift their aspirations. Often this leads to very significant changes in the basis for their self-esteem. This normal process began with Robertson, but he cut it short by his retreat. He felt he could not tolerate the anxiety and depression of his sophomore year. He thought the institute was indifferent to his plight. Rather than continue to re-evaluate his ideals in terms of science, he retreated and regrouped his forces and saved his reserves for a different battle. It is reasonable to speculate whether he might have worked out a different solution if the institution had made fewer demands on his energy and time during the crises. Had he been able to find paths between the scientific and nonscientific universes, he might have been able to make it. He said as a senior that he thought this might have been possible.

Listening to students, one notes how readily they link their evaluation of their worth as individuals and their image of themselves to their experience at school. Thus, Moore saw himself as competent, quietly caring for his classmates and his friends, and valued his willingness to take risks in the academic game. Jones took pride in "winning" with respect to the academic structure. He was proud of his skill in figuring out and in using that skill to beat the system. He felt good about himself because he was "number one." Smith was able to maintain his image of himself as having a special, magically potent intellect, as long as he could ignore the fact of his academic failure. Brown learned the syllabi of both curricula and used the time gained to pursue his special interests in depth. Robertson saw his worth as an individual resting in significant measure on his caring for his younger classmates, those in more distress than he. He maintained his sense of competence to some extent by avoiding risks, and derived self-satisfaction from working the syllabi well.

Selective negligence, dedication to purposefulness, and setting the inner clock by the institutional clock were all tasks of M.I.T.'s hidden curriculum at a particular point in its history. Today, in a new decade, these tasks have changed significantly or are still undergoing redefinition.

On other campuses the tasks are not necessarily the same. Selective negligence may be replaced by diligent attention to all details. The tasks of the hidden curriculum became crucial for these students because mastery of these tasks came to be the criterion by which these students judged their worth. They viewed themselves in these terms because this is how they saw themselves regarded by their faculty. Thus the students' self-esteem became linked to an institutional process.

The social setting in which these tasks are embedded appeared to put a premium on certain specific adaptive responses on the part of students, a penalty on others. Consider the degree to which the individual student can tolerate anxiety, the extent to which he can still function effectively while terrified of failure.

Smith (and the others like him) had not understood the tasks of the hidden curriculum. He tried to "know it all" because the good feeling that he associated with knowing it all was his way of protecting himself from his primitive anxiety of knowing nothing—that is, being helpless and impotent. For some students, even the fear of failure triggered a shift in their image of themselves from strong to weak. When Smith felt a diminished sense of worth, he became even less able to mobilize himself, to act, and tried to avoid his depression and feeling of helplessness with a fantasy of a brilliant, magical brain. Smith illustrates the cycle of an adaptive failure: Anxiety over his ability to succeed led him to deny the anxiety;

NEGLIGENCE, COMPETENCE, COMMITMENT

thus he could not stop and look around long enough to see what was going wrong. Instead he retreated into imagined competence and withdrew further from the scene.

Some students live and function well with a level of almost constant tension that others find incapacitating. The problem for students (and for all of us), however, is not only how much anxiety can we stand, but the range of defenses against anxiety available in a particular environment as we attempt to cope with its presence; and within that range, the specific ways of coping that different students adopt. Some defenses, as we saw with Smith, dampen the anxiety at the same time that the range of stimuli to which the student can respond is dramatically curtailed. The student who is made anxious by looking at the scene before him may well feel calm again by closing his eyes; the ostrich is the model. But such a response means almost certain failure. There may be settings where such a response is useful. A university, however, should not be one.

The question that recurs constantly is: Does the institution affect the student's choice of defenses against anxiety, the pattern of adaptation, and if so, by what means?

An answer came from an academically successful senior who reflected on the way the institute rewarded him with A's, with offers for special assignments because he was so "well organized, because I can do the things that need to be done so well. I'm just beginning to see that I turn off my feeling for Jane, ignore her, she says, when I'm working, doing what my project or professor expects. She's right to say I'm a stranger at just those times when the professor says 'great work,' and it's easier. It's more than that, that's even why I'm here at school, to find out if I can do those things. But I wonder—why can't I feel more, care more where Jane's at when my work is going well?" His anxiety about grades had long since passed, and his conscious uneasiness about dating Jane had, for at least a year, been replaced or supplanted by only a mild irritation that the time with her was time away from work.

This theme, present in a number of the students as they move through their undergraduate years, has emerged with even greater emphasis in recent interviews with the students, four years after graduation, who had mastered selective negligence early, while still freshmen. In addition, by Christmas of the freshman year, most, if not all, of these successful students had adjusted their sense of time to the institution's clock. One graduate student, for example, put it this way:

> From the beginning I found the whole thing to be a kind of exercise in time budgeting. I found during my first year that I was very worried about it not being possible to do everything that every course asked you to do. You had to filter out what was really important in each course, regardless of whether you were worried about the grade or not. You couldn't physically do it all. I found out that if you did a good job of filtering out what was

important you could do well enough to do well in every course.

I like to think that those professors knew very well what they were doing, that they knew very well that the people weren't going to do it all, but were offering the stuff as a guide to what you might do.

This student enjoyed his ability to work the way he did. His sense of being worthwhile was increasingly derived, first, from his actual mastery of the content of his courses, as reflected in high grades, and, second, on the adaptive stance associated with that mastery. His means to this end:

> I think one of the things that made me happy about the place is that I did feel there was a connection between whether you learned anything and whether you did well. The effect on me, at least, was not bad—the effect of the fact that you did have to budget and couldn't do everything and the fact that there was this pressure for grades. I was learning a great deal by doing things this way. I was maintaining my efficiency for learning in pretty good shape by not trying to do everything. I was very happy (after freshman year) because I did have this feeling very often of delight at really figuring things out, how things worked.

By its reward structure, by the fashion in which it poses the task itself, obliquely or with precision, the institution appeared to sanction denial rather than acknowledgment of anxiety as its preferred mode of response. Where the institution has a significant, though not necessarily determining, effect on the "acceptable" response to anxiety (or to love, or anger, or work), the consequences of the hidden curriculum come to have a dramatic and profound impact on the student's emotional as well as intellectual development. Some students are able to work effectively only at the expense of their ability to care. They come to rely on their skill in budgeting their time, their emotions, their degree of commitment to such an extent that their sense of competence and worth as individuals is threatened if their budget goes awry.

3

DISTRACTION AND THE EXPROPRIATION OF LEARNING
Martin Trow[1]

> *I think [the students] are so busy doing something all the time doing a set kind of task, and in courses they are so busy memorizing and taking exams, that we stifle what is a very important quality, which is to be boss of your subject. . . . I would say that the process of undergraduate learning is much too passive . . . and for that reason, is very different from what will ultimately be expected of you—the kind of role that you'll ultimately play in life.*
> —A Professor

The faculty, observing their relationships with their students, see the various sources of stress for their students

---

[1] Professor of Sociology in the Graduate School of Public Affairs, University of California, Berkeley. He is the author of many articles on

and for themselves. Focusing on stresses and strains in higher education is, however, misleading if we do not also point to the resources of imagination that such institutions can bring to bear on their problems. The tensions described in this chapter are aspects of life at M.I.T., even five years after the interviewing on which these findings are largely based. But awareness of these tensions, especially as they affect student life, has led to certain reforms[2] of the undergraduate curriculum that are designed to mitigate some of the problems. And these reforms are still in progress, even as new problems and difficulties arise in the life of the Institute and its faculty which we could scarcely have anticipated or even imagined five years ago.

British and American higher education. His newest book is *The British Academics,* written in collaboration with A. H. Halsey (London: Faber and Faber). Professor Trow is also Director of the National Survey of Higher Education sponsored by the Carnegie Commission on Higher Education. He has been a consultant to the project at M.I.T. since 1963. This chapter is based on a relatively small number of intensive interviews with M.I.T. faculty members, together with informal conversations and observations during visits over a five-year period.

[2] Some of these reforms have been directed at elements of the "hidden curriculum" which were identified and discussed in Chapters 1 and 2. Among these is an increase in elective courses in the first two years; the more frequent provision of courses graded on a pass-fail basis which do not affect the cumulative grade-point average; the wider availability of tutorials to undergraduates; and the tendency to separate scholarship support awarded on admission from the maintenance of a specific "cum." Nevertheless, these reforms have not changed the basic climate of the institution, or the basic patterns of stress in the faculty-student relationship discussed in this chapter by Professor Trow.

DISTRACTION AND EXPROPRIATION

Though M.I.T. has certain special characteristics, the issues discussed are clearly recognizable in other major universities, even if details differ. The Institute has a demanding curriculum which dominates a large part of the student's working hours. Its severe selectivity insures that it admits only highly able and, on the whole, highly motivated students. As discussed in Chapters 1 and 2, the demands it makes, and the rewards it offers, both in the present and in promise, have profound effects on the lives of students.

Universities also generate peculiar pressures on and difficulties for their faculties. These vary in different parts of a college or university, in different departments, as well as at different levels of rank and authority. The demands made on the faculty, the resources at their disposal, and their own intellectual and emotional capacities for coping, together comprise a major component of the environment in which the student functions. To put it in highly abbreviated form: if the faculty has great difficulty in performing its roles, in meeting the explicit and implicit demands made on it, then difficulties will be experienced by its students in ways that may interfere with their education—with their intellectual, moral, and emotional growth.

The student is exhorted to be creative and imaginative, to take risks, to strike out boldly and take responsibility for his own education and his own intellectual development. These are the goals of academic science: the creative man for whom what is known is merely the precipitate of a process of inquiry which is more important than the corpus of knowledge. On the other hand, the student is confronted in all his courses with enormous masses of material to be learned, and for the most part, however he is exhorted, he is graded on his capacity to master the body of knowledge—on his competence rather than on his creativity.

This concern for competence lies behind the work overload and the expropriation of leisure that are the most immediately visible marks of difference between M.I.T. and liberal arts colleges. As one professor of engineering observed:

> There is this fear that somehow the person will get through us deficient in some major regard, and I'm sure that we're worried in two regards—one is that we are worried that we will not produce a good product . . . making mechanical engineers. And this is a matter of pride and a matter of responsibility. And then [there is the] fear that the student may himself get into trouble, may fail, may perform an operation and not succeed. And then there's always this cult of magic in the sense that mechanical engineers should know certain things.

A major source of strain at M.I.T. lies in its dual character as a "university polarized around science" and a professional school for engineers.[3] As a university, it centers on the basic academic disciplines, especially the sciences, and on the creation of knowledge and the preparation of students to teach the disciplines and contribute to the fund of knowledge. The qualities it most highly rewards are those associated with the creation of knowledge: originality and creativity. But M.I.T. is also a professional school, and the qualities that professional schools in particular must stress are not only brilliance or creativity, but competence. Important is the ability to do a job, a job that by and large lies outside the Institute and is defined and judged by others in the practicing professions and in industrial organizations. The essence of creativity, on the other hand, is the ability to contribute to a body of knowledge in ways that are prescribed by the academic disciplines themselves; it is scientists who decide what science is, how to advance it, and what constitutes a creative contribution.

The tensions between these two roles or missions of the Institute are reflected in the conflicting demands that the faculty makes of students.

There is then still the belief that if one only puts a little

[3] In the academic year 1968–9, 1,276 undergraduate and graduate degrees were awarded. These degrees were distributed among the five schools as follows: 632 from the School of Engineering, 324 from the School of Science, 161 from the Sloan School of Management, 101 from the School of Humanities and Social Science, and 36 from the School of Architecture and Planning.

more into the curriculum, the engineer will be a little less inadequate, despite the increasing recognition among engineers at M.I.T., as elsewhere, that it is really quite impossible to prepare an engineer in all the necessary ways in four years. In fact, 80 percent of M.I.T. graduates now go on to graduate school or other advanced training; thus, only a minority must be prepared to exercise professional competence after four years. Under conditions of rapid technological change and growth of knowledge, the effort to produce competent engineers in four years involves the effort to transmit large amounts of skill and knowledge. The volume of knowledge organized in the curriculum, which constantly encroaches on leisure, exercises a kind of tyranny over the student which largely precludes his taking time to develop or pursue his own intellectual interests, even when they are closely related to his professional training.

Work overload and the expropriation of leisure is recognized by almost everybody; periodically, the faculty makes a study and agrees to try to reduce the course load, but to no avail. Whatever the nominal number of credit hours assigned to courses, they inexorably increase their content to fill, and more than fill, the student's day.

At least some faculty members see the curriculum as directly antithetical to the qualities of mind of a creative scholar. As one professor put it:

DISTRACTION AND EXPROPRIATION

I'm thinking mainly now of the first two years, when the students really get started at M.I.T. and shaped. The individual departments operate in a traditional pattern, the format of which is too authoritarian to my way of thinking, although the individuals aren't. There is a lot of memorization and this business of freshman quizzes, in a different subject once every week, and the students just immediately get into what for me is the antithesis of the kind of opening, exciting, intellectual experience that they should be getting.

M.I.T. was more like a vocational high school thirty years ago than it is now, and you could say to a student, "All right, go take an hour of engineering drawing, and then rush over here and learn these skills. . . ." But now, within that same format, with a lot of momentum from this earlier pattern, you're asking students to carry out serious and demanding intellectual exercises. And the students are extremely good. This is something that most of the faculty doesn't recognize—it doesn't adequately recognize its extremely able students.

I think another feature—and this is an important one—is that our education is in the form of undergraduate professional education. . . . Those are just words, but words influence the way people think of themselves, and so on. For example, . . . some of our engineering departments are restricted and prevented from giving the best kind of education they could give, simply because they are self-consciously concerned with the fact that they are producing students who are officially such-and-such a kind of engineer, and accredited as such, etc., etc. . . . It says so on his degree . . . but it really doesn't. This is the paradox: all the students go on to graduate school . . . so that in an ironic way, the work that the departments do is still being dominated by perhaps 20 percent of the students who don't go on to graduate school.

I noticed a very noticeable difference when I came here from Harvard, and the kind of question that I asked I've heard asked by other people, and it's a fine thing. What I said to myself was, "Here I've been at Harvard, where in a junior- or senior-level course of thirty students, maybe four or five of them would get really interested. The rest would do the work, but the four or five who were really interested, were *really* interested, and they'd go off for two days and do nothing but work on some remark that I had made in class or so, or anything that I suggested would be interesting to look at." So I got this feeling that at least some students were sort of able to marshal their forces and be interested in something that interested them. Here, after about two months, I was saying, "What's wrong? There's something wrong," and then I realized what was wrong, and that is that no one was getting really interested in what I was doing in class. They were responding and taking the quizzes, but where were the students who would come up with their eyes shining and full of excitement and be interested? They weren't there. Why not? *Too much to do.*

At the same time, one has to keep in mind that the faculty at M.I.T., by and large, is pretty good, and as

DISTRACTION AND EXPROPRIATION

individuals they're very good, so, say, our students in mathematics or physics or whatever—they're sort of caught in this system which is demanding too much of them; at the same time the quality of the material they're getting is very good, and the individual teacher may sort of try to fight this in a very imaginative way. So that you do get some very good individual intellectual experiences. The problem comes with a given student in the over-all scene where he has just too much to do. The students take No-Doz tablets and, getting five hours sleep a night, just drive themselves from one thing to another. This may be an exaggerated picture, but that's no way to become a good scientist.

It is not only the whip of the overload curriculum, but also the carrot of praise for high competence which tends to interfere with the student's finding his own voice and unique talent. One scientist put it this way:

This premium [at M.I.T.] on the measured achievement which gives the constant rewards probably means that any except the real oddball will be seduced into putting his effort in that direction. Now in that sense . . . M.I.T. has always been that way, and engineering schools have always been that way—perhaps rightly so because it is probably what you want to educate for: conformity. [But] now you seduce the people away. You don't bluff them, you don't bury them—this kind of thing I don't think you can bury by too much work—but you can probably seduce a fellow away by giving him too much of a premium for being clever in the competence sense. You know, you find it takes rather a sophisticated fellow who will say, "Yes, I could probably cover myself with glory with a straight A average, but why should I?"

He was asked if he and his colleagues were able to offer any counter rewards for eccentricity or uniqueness, for *not* playing the game as it is defined by the Institution. The professor's reply sheds some light on the difficulties of nurturing the unique voice under conditions of mass higher education even in the most highly selective institutions:

> You know, there's only one way of doing that. You have to really like people. . . . Now the question is, do we love our students enough? That is a terrible way of saying it, but I mean it in the real sense. Well, I certainly don't. I'm not that kind of person. I think by and large in the physical sciences you will find that you have a selection of people who don't, because there is a thing that attracts them into the field. One teaches by example, of course. *But whether one can like the fellow who doesn't understand what you are saying because he is thinking in his own terms—that's hard.*[4] There are some people who do, and I guess they're great teachers. . . . Now do we make it especially hard? Yes, of course we do, because the numbers are large. We aren't creating this, [but] it was much

[4] Emphasis supplied.

DISTRACTION AND EXPROPRIATION

easier when the students were hard to come by. Now I will say one thing: We have made real progress over what the situation was when I was a student, because of the greater competence that they [present day students] acquire. We can take the seniors into the lab, so I think we're getting them as undergraduates to the point of real contact. Now the contact is probably a little diluted because there are more of them, but it's earlier and that may really help.

This man went on to observe that he could only help a student find his own voice in science "by working with a fellow long enough so that I'm really beginning to be personally interested in *him,* not in education in abstract terms." And that happens very rarely between him and undergraduates, and never before the senior year. For this distinguished professor, at least, all the rest of the undergraduate education at M.I.T. was a training for conformity, for the high competence that to him was the antithesis of the man's own unique voice and the discovery of his own unique talent.

This respondent makes in passing an extremely important point: that the encouragement of intellectual nonconformity and, by implication, creativity requires a personal relationship between teacher and student of a kind that is not required for training in conformity, even to high levels of competence. And the personal relationship necessary to "like the fellow who doesn't understand what you are saying because he is thinking in his own terms" is precluded by the heavy demands of a required curriculum and discouraged by the large number of students. (And for this kind of distinguished professor it is also impossible if the student does not already have a sufficiently high level of competence in the subject to allow fruitful communication.) But we get a glimpse here of creativity among students. The question is, Does the curriculum, and indeed the structure of the institution, allow for the kind of personal relationships with faculty members that permit students to find their own voice and unique qualities? There is a great deal of research which purports to show that there is no relationship between, say, class size or faculty-student ratios and academic performance. But when we are talking about intellectual performance at its highest level, as this respondent, an eminent scientist himself, is doing, then we realize that this research and its findings depend on measures of achievement that may not measure the growth of those qualities of mind that are associated with genuine creative achievement.

What we are being told by the faculty respondents is that the relationships which nurture creative qualities of mind are rare in undergraduate education, and at best occur in the graduate training. It is an important question, both for reflection and policy, whether the emphasis on competence in undergraduate training in education while allowing creative work to survive as best it can until postgraduate years is indeed a sound and defensible educational strategy. But it is only fair to suggest that the alternatives are likely to be expensive, and perhaps prohibitively so, particularly in the education of scientists and technologists.[5]

The differences between the demands and conditions appropriate for creativity and for competence show themselves in a number of ways. Faculty members see overload as incompatible with the cultivation of creative capacities and yet required by the increasing volumes of knowledge needed for competence. On the other hand there is the persistent belief that first-rate minds cannot be hurt by anything the university does, nor deflected by any set of organizational conditions. Some faculty members believed that really first-rate people show themselves despite the constraints of the curriculum and of work overload; there were many echoes to the assertion of one physicist that "the really great creative minds will come through in any case." And for those who believe this, the question of the organization of the curriculum or of other institutional conditions becomes a question of how to enable competent people to function at a somewhat more effective level. The conviction that quality will out in the face of any discouragement tends to allow many faculty

---

[5] But this perhaps exaggerates the incompatibility of training for competence and for creativity. In Chapter 7 the author suggests the need for different kinds of encounters between students, opportunities for them to work together in a genuine apprenticeship relationship that might reconcile the need to transmit skills and the need to encourage unique talents.

members—notably the pure scientists—to withhold their strongest interests from the curriculum and institutional reform because finally these are peripheral matters to men whose deepest concerns are with the handful of first-rate minds among their students. As one physicist put it, "I'm not worried about losing the great ones [among the students], but there might be some very good ones who will only be very good on a lower level [given existing institutional practices]."

From this perspective—which is the perspective of many elite scientists—the overload of the curriculum is at the same time a product of the pressure for competence and an obstacle to competence at its highest level of performance. In this view, real creativity is independent of conditions and cannot be planned for or aborted. It has almost a mystical quality of being out of time and place: it is very rare, it is unquenchable, and ultimately it is what makes the whole enterprise worthwhile. That view, so deeply held by the most prestigious members of the faculty, has many consequences, not least of which is the way it communicates itself to the student body. Insofar as students accept its conception of academic work and achievement, it makes most of them second-class citizens and requires a negative self-evaluation of those who do not define themselves as absolutely first-class. In a sense, universities place enormous emphasis in their organizational practices on the acquisition of high competence. Its leading men speak of it, however, as "merely" competence, and this cannot but be a source of strain and difficulty for the ordinary student who is not a Rutherford or an Einstein, or a T. S. Eliot, and knows it.

Elitist educational systems are very hard on their students; they sponsor them, they surround them with the best of facilities, they give them close personal attention and nurture their gifts, but finally they make severe judgments on the majority of them. In British universities, which certainly are as highly selective as the most selective American universities, one hears from even the ablest students expressions of self-depreciation and of not having lived up to some standard set for them by their instructors. Indeed, the severest self-judgments are made by extremely able students who earn good second-class degrees but fall just short of earning first-class honors in the British university. And this may also be the case at the most academically prestigious American universities. The opposite side of the coin is that in such universities rare gifts are constantly being sought for and are likely to be identified. These universities also create an environment in which all the students can imagine themselves to be members of an elite whose brightest ornament is the occasional gifted creative man. The question is whether a university oriented to the rare and highly gifted person must necessarily create an environment quite so punishing to the others, who, though extremely able, do not possess the extraordinary qualities that characterize the tiny elite within the elite. Robert Oppenheimer was once asked on television whether he thought the expansion of the physical sciences had adversely affected the education of the nearly ten thousand undergraduate and graduate students then majoring in physics. He smiled at the questioner and said, "Well, to tell the truth, I don't know anything about that. I'm really only interested in about ten of them." Something of that spirit is present at many elite universities and is part of the climate for all of their students and faculty.[6]

Another important feature of elite universities is the competition between departments and men for the best students.

The movement of students into and out of courses is affected by the long-range changes in science and technology which increase the relevance and demands for some fields as they reduce that of others.[7] The relative decline of certain branches of engineering reflects those changes: for example, some subjects which were the centers of lively research and had many students twenty

---

[6] But only part of the climate. There is at M.I.T., for example, a strong interest among leading scientists in the general state of scientific education, and not just in the "top ten." Among these countercurrents are the notable contributions of Jerrold Zacharias and his colleagues to the physics curriculum in secondary schools and the work of Professors French, King, Valley, Schein, etc.

But this interest of some leading men at M.I.T. in "mass" scientific education does not contradict the strong elitist values of the Institute as a whole to which Trow is pointing.

[7] For a fuller discussion of student movement in and out of courses see Chapter 6, p. 146.

DISTRACTION AND EXPROPRIATION

years ago have been greatly and suddenly affected by the development of high-speed computers; others are affected more gradually by developments in other fields which draw away their intellectual excitement, research support, and thus students. And the rate of growth of scientific and technological knowledge is so high that for individual men, as well as for whole areas of work, there is a constant threat of obsolescence or decline of relevance and attractiveness to students.

These developments have momentous consequences for faculty members in science and engineering: for their prestige and status, which are so closely linked to that of their subjects, for their morale, and for their relations with their students. One administrative officer spoke of a department which "ten or fifteen years ago had well over a hundred undergraduates in each year. Now it has sixteen." And he went on to speak of seeing "the dismay and shattered morale" of that department as its student numbers declined, along with its technological relevance, leading to "all kinds of unhappy situations—personal recriminations. . . ." But while student numbers decline, the men remain, in one capacity or another, part of the stressful environment for all students who come in contact with them in whatever capacity.

The competition for students and the consequences of that competition on the students can be seen throughout the Institute and not only in those departments suffering the effects of technological obsolescence. At M.I.T., for instance, the institution controls the number of graduate students in any department, but not the number of undergraduate students, who, in a sense, "vote with their feet," both in their initial choice of courses and through transfers.[8] As a result, in the words of one administrative officer:

> The students set policy, and it's very dangerous.
> [How?]
> Because as faculties compete for students, the poor students get torn between them.
> [Why?]
> This place is so pledged to quality that they [the faculty] take the stand that all students will seek out the most challenging course. . . . As I look at some of these M.I.T. students, they get so keyed up during the academic year that it takes them weeks to decompress.

The department's reputation, and thus its drawing power, depends in part on its reputation for being tough, by offering "the most challenging course." This creates a continual source of increasing demand on the students, who, having internalized the university's standards and values, respond by demanding more and more of them-

[8] Departments do exercise some degree of *informal* control over the numbers and character of their students through their grading, their counseling, and the kinds of courses they offer. See Chapter 6, p. 146.

DISTRACTION AND EXPROPRIATION

selves. Students at less selective institutions are much more likely not to take the demands of the faculty so seriously —to remain psychologically at a distance from them. This reduces the impact of the institution, but for some students it also increases freedom.

Another professor links the competition for the students and for their time with work overload and routinization. Asked whether students have to be governed and supervised so closely, whether they couldn't be given more responsibility for their own education, he replied:

> Well, I think this would be a wonderful thing, if we could first work it out. Now, I don't drive my students hard, I don't drive myself hard. There are people who do, and when I find here that my students spend their time working on somebody else's course because I haven't driven them hard, this is extremely annoying to me. When one fellow has a course which he lists in the catalog as a twelve-hour course and actually it takes twenty, and the students work twenty hours on his course and then neglect mine, . . . this bothers me . . . and I don't know what to do about it.
>
> [Do some people react by making their own courses tougher in retaliation?]
>
> I think this is what everybody does, and this comes right on top of the students. And of course if you do this, you're much more likely to ask mathematical questions which have simple answers. . . . It's much easier to in-

crease the load if you can correct the problems; . . . and I think . . . this is why we drive our students, because we do compete for [their] time.

Part of the pressure on students arises from an austere work ethic deeply embedded in the values and personalities of many faculty members. One professor suggests something of the nature of these pressures:

> You could never say it's a relaxed atmosphere here. It's not a relaxed atmosphere, it's a very heavy work-oriented atmosphere. There's a tendency for each of us who deal with freshmen—a very ready tendency, I think—to be concerned about their understanding what we are now saying to them, doing for them, working with them, as opposed to being at least as interested in some other course than our own and [their] success in that and to be, hopefully, interested in whether they are personally learning anything and enjoying themselves in this experience. I don't think that any of us contribute as much as we might in this regard. There's a tendency somehow to feel that what *we* are doing for this boy is more important than what everybody will do for him and what he is doing in response to this.
>
> [Do you think there is any acute difficulty about overload and stress?]
>
> . . . I cannot use myself as an example because my Dad drove me during various times of my life into really almost superhuman situations for which my own chil-

dren suffer, because, if I don't watch out, I can easily expect too much of anybody, simply because I wouldn't hesitate to expect it of myself. . . . This finally becomes a kind of lifelong habit. . . . You don't mind it any more.

But [speaking of the students] because of the work habit, the study habit thing, this is all part of a much bigger problem, which is mainly a failure to account for time —to have a running commitment and an understanding of how much time they've spent. The ones that you could see, [time] was their trouble—whole hours of the week just disappearing—they didn't know what had happened. [I've encouraged them to] just keep a time budget for one week, to keep it down to the level of five minutes for one week, and then to try to budget the next week. If you can anticipate what commitments you're going to make to various subjects and activities of all sorts in a journal—then you can see how bad your guess was at the end of the week. My advice to students is to try to do this in such a way that at least one evening a week there's no committed plan in advance, so that if a group were going up to the country for a weekend or skiing or something you really want to do, that's it, you do it. On the other hand, you only do it once a week. You've now spent this period of time . . . a genuine budget.

[Tell me, did you do something like this when you were here?]

Yeah, but I didn't have to do it consciously, because I had been encouraged to do the same kind of thing since I was ten years old—I had a built-in kind of clock.

THE HIDDEN CURRICULUM

The effects of overload and the expropriation of leisure are seen vividly and directly in the student interviews. Here we can see some of the sources of these pressures among the faculty, arising in part out of the vocational-school tradition, in part out of a work ethic among Institute faculty that makes hard work a virtue in itself, almost independent of its effect on a student's education, and in part out of status insecurities of departments struggling for survival and more, or better, students. In this milieu, even a demonstrated connection between more "leisure" and a less directed form of instruction on one hand, and more creative students on the other, probably would not affect the climate of learning and instruction: it is built not on misinformation but into the men and the institution which sets the tasks and administers the rewards and punishments.

One professor sees the matter this way:

> I think that the first year at M.I.T., the students are under too much pressure. I think there is too much expected of them. [What form does this pressure take, and what effect do you think it has on the students getting into the world of science?] Well, one of the reactions that one gets is that they study all the time without thinking. They . . . become mechanical. I mean they have a certain amount to do; and when you give them an opportunity to take it a little less rigorously, they do nothing.

DISTRACTION AND EXPROPRIATION

The professor went on to observe that he himself tries not to push his freshmen quite so hard, but rather gives them more responsibility for organizing their own work:

> I'd never make specific homework assignments. . . . But I tried to present it to them in the sense that this is the material you can use to check your achievement against. Do you know the material? Do you understand it? But I'm not going to ask you to turn in problem 8 on Wednesday morning at ten o'clock, but you should work enough of these problems on your own to see whether you can cope with it, and if you have trouble I expect you to bring it up in discussion and recitation or see me in conference hour and we'll go over it and try to get it straightened out. And the usual reaction to this is that if it isn't specifically assigned, they don't do it. And this doesn't bother me too much because it's their own neck that's being hurt, and I'm willing and want to help them as much as possible, but I feel that sooner or later they have to develop the business of taking the initiative on this, because I always tell my students I can't teach them a damn thing. I can help them learn it.

This same professor further observed, however, that when the pressure is lightened in one course or department, it tends to be increased elsewhere.

> I don't know if anything could be done about that or not. I do feel that it's not just the institution, but it's the

faculty-student interaction, the fact that we do get good students in here, that the students are capable of doing work, but you try to set up the work so that you get sort of a normal distribution in their performance, and so the better the students, the higher the standards go, and the more work there is. Unfortunately, I think part of this pressure is on quantity and not necessarily on quality. And this has become a pattern because there has been an increase in the capabilities of the students that we're getting, there's no question about it.

A powerful and pervasive motive of academic men in leading institutions is their ambition for national recognition—for themselves, for their departments and subjects, and for their institutions. These academic reputations are rooted in scholarly and scientific research; it is affected very slightly by a man's reputation as a teacher or colleague, or anything else. In federal grant universities, many other considerations tend to be subordinated to status in a national or international pecking order.

Academic ambition has a profound influence on the institutional climate. One dean at M.I.T. spoke of the frenetic pace of change and of the need to "calm the place down somehow":

> Now you can only calm a place down, it seems to me, by somehow or other relaxing many of the aspirations, and these would be the aspirations of the institution itself to

DISTRACTION AND EXPROPRIATION

maintain its position. So when you're Number One, you hate to become Number Two. It's terrible. Just think of me. Can I possibly face up to the fact that during my tenure as academic dean, my school slipped from first place to second place? No, it's ridiculous. And secondly, it's also important to remember that the lead we have isn't anything one can become complacent about, because I know many of my colleagues in other schools look upon M.I.T. as Number One, but they think they're going to jockey us out of that. You can't let your guard down very long.

It is quite unlikely that universities will "calm down" by relaxing many of their aspirations; certainly this dean was not prepared to.

The dean was speaking here of the strain of striving for institutional status in a relentlessly competitive academic world full of schools that want to "jockey us out of first place." But institutional and individual status and aspirations are closely linked—and both increase stress on the undergraduates.[9] Setting a very high standard for an institution is an aspect of the milieu which is quickly absorbed by the students. Indeed, for many at M.I.T., it was why they came. And for many of the teachers and their students, work, unremitting work, is an unqualified

---

[9] There is a clear parallel between this dean's sense of never-ending competitive threat from other institutions and the fear of many students that to "let down" would result in disaster to their own academic standing in M.I.T.

virtue and a sure way to achieve recognition and high distinction—one is almost tempted to say salvation.

Another major source of faculty stress at major universities arises out of *systematic distraction*—the disruption of a man's work and thought by frequent demands on his attention from others. A variety of factors have significantly increased the number and range of the faculty member's activities, and thus of the people who have some claim on his time and attention. Faculty members are widely involved as consultants to federal, state, and local governments and private business; many are deeply enmeshed in large-scale research projects involving other people and considerable administration; they are active in a host of national and international professional associations; they are involved in almost continuous reassessment of the organization and content of the educational programs at their institutions; and they have students. Almost all their activities are undergoing growth and change, which involves continual consultation and discussion. For example, the growth in federal support for basic and applied research and development in science and technology grew from less than 1 billion dollars in 1948 to over 16 billion in 1968.[1]

[1] As the leading technical and scientific university in the country (one third of its students are in humanities and social science), M.I.T. has had far more than a proportionate share in the spending of these funds, and in providing consultants for managing and allocating them to others. And currently the Institute is ramifying its activities beyond the traditional spheres of science and technology into new problem areas—the city, transportation, health, education.

DISTRACTION AND EXPROPRIATION

The basic source of distraction for a faculty member lies in the growth in the number of people who have a "legitimate" claim on his attention,[2] without any concomitant change in the norms which govern a man's relations with his colleagues. The norms of scholarship require a relatively free exchange of information; moreover, they presuppose that within the very broad fraternity of scholars, men will be as helpful as possible to others who seek their aid in the pursuit of some legitimate professional enterprise. It is, in short, difficult to say "no" to a request for aid or information—and extremely difficult when such requests are made by genuine colleagues in one's own discipline elsewhere or in any discipline in one's own institution. The norms governing a man's responsiveness to requests for help from colleagues arose when the world and universities were much smaller; they persist as the most powerful moral forces in scholarship when that world is much larger. The result is that the commonest complaint, at every large university, is of an academic man's difficulty in doing his own work in the face of constant distraction by others.

Faculty complaints about distraction are marked by a sense of hopelessness and of helplessness to stem the tide. During one interview, a professor of engineering gestured

[2] In 1948–9, 126 people earned doctoral degrees in mathematics in American universities; in 1966–7 the number was 832. In physics the comparable figures were 266 (1948–9) and 1,183 (1966–7). In all fields of engineering the number of doctorates rose from 494 to 2,614 between 1949–50 and 1966–7.

out of the window toward a new building being erected a short distance away on the campus:

> See that? In a few months it will be finished and filled with people—and they're all going to want to talk to me.

And indeed, there is very little exaggeration in his complaint. On inquiry, it was clear that the building would be housing many scientists and research men whose work would indeed lead a large number of them to seek the advice and help of my informant, and there was no way he could see of dealing with their requests except by talking to them.

Another professor in a science discipline put it this way:

> There's nobody who has guts enough to say "no"—that this is a wonderful project but we're not going to do it. And the reason we're not going to do it is that we've got a lot of other things to do. Every project that comes along, everybody says yes, we'll do it. . . . You get torn to bits trying to get scattered out into such small pieces. [So that in your own experience there's a rapidly increasing series of demands on your own time and attention?] That's right, . . . just insignificant little things, but so many of them.
>
> Well, the worst thing I find is this—I've got so used to interruptions that I can no longer give anything my close attention for a long period of time. . . . When I do have the time, I can't use it that way and I have to produce

DISTRACTION AND EXPROPRIATION

interruptions because I've just gotten used to it. And the result is that I don't get anything done. It's a horrible situation—we've really been trained to be scattered all over the place . . . and you see this is really the function of the kind of unlimited possibilities of doing everything.

The department head, he has some new ideas, comes in, says, "Gee, this is a wonderful idea, let's get some people together and we'll talk about it." So we get some people together. Millions of these things. . . . As the number of people increases with whom we have contact, the conversation increases in much more than direct ratio because the number of possible lines of communication increases extraordinarily rapidly with the number of people, so that as the organization gets bigger you finally get to the point where there is no output and only conversation. We're approaching this point quite rapidly.

Another professor finds his distractions taking the form of a demanding committee on the form of the undergraduate curriculum. And he saw the problem as arising out of his own "failings"—his sense of responsibility to the institution and his inability to say "no."

In my own personal case, I've got involved with a variety of responsibilities in the Institute outside the department, and I feel I lead a life of quiet desperation on this score. . . . But it's my own fault and it's not something I have to do, it's something that I just got entangled in and so I feel, I guess somebody has to do it, and it's worth doing.

THE HIDDEN CURRICULUM

. . . But I'm not very good at saying "no," and I get along pretty well with my colleagues in the department and I get along pretty well with people outside the department. . . . [Thus] for the first time, this is really where I've gotten entangled a little bit—for the first time I had responsibilities which were not associated with the department in any direct way. . . . It's thrown off a lot of my energy in the last year.

Perhaps the most poignant account of the effects of distraction was provided by a brilliant scientist who is uncommonly sensitive to the effects of the social environment on his own creative capacities.

M.I.T. is a place which, for one thing, encourages and breeds, tremendously successfully, competence. [But] it is an almost impossible place to go through the full creative cycle. I have a sort of quick aphoristic way of describing this. I say the trouble with M.I.T. is you can never work through your depression properly. You know, you do a piece of work with your full commitment and it goes through the full peaking and then [comes] the postpartum depression. And now you go around with that depression, with the feeling, "I will never do anything useful again in my life and that's the end," and that is when the ideas germinate and then slowly it goes again. At M.I.T. there's a real danger that when you walk down the corridor at that stage, somebody dashes out the door and says, "Look, we've got a *terribly* exciting project. We *need* you, can't you possibly come and spare some time

DISTRACTION AND EXPROPRIATION

and help us?" And this is a crucial thing for the world, for the country, for science and what not. And at that stage you can't risk that. Now you're going to do a lot of good, but that idea which was going to grow while you were down there at the bottom will never come to fruition.

This scientist went on to suggest that he believes that for the creative scientist the characteristic pattern is "the manic-depressive—I don't mean that in quite the clinical sense, but it is with the creative upsurge and bubbling and then with a slump. . . ." And he felt that it was precisely the numbers of interesting people and projects at the Institute that tended to abort the natural cycle of creation depression and the slow painful climb toward an active interest in some new problem, when an expression of interest by others catches a man just at the moment when he is most vulnerable, when he believes or fears he will never do anything very good again.

The distraction and overload these men speak of surely have large consequences for their research work and their teaching. It is the latter, of course, that we are concerned with here. It is difficult to demonstrate these effects, to show just how the constant ringing of the phone, the frequent callers at the door, create tensions which the teacher brings into the classroom with him and which, in that or other indirect ways, become part of the students' stressful environment. And of course the balance sheet is not all in red: the teacher's position on the frontier of his discipline, his involvement in large and exciting plans and projects, enrich as well as subvert the climate of learning he creates for his students. But we are concerned here not with all the components of the students' environment, but particularly with those which cause him special difficulties in his own patterns of response and accommodation. And among these, the climate of distraction and overload in which his teachers work becomes part of his own world of pressure and stress.[3]

New kinds of stress in the student-faculty relationship have emerged in recent years as part of the current political upheavals in American higher education which did not appear in these interviews, but are now clearly present at all major universities.

One of these arises out of the marked increase of student participation in decision-making at all levels of the university. In meetings of departments and schools, and on committees and commissions at every level, students are increasingly represented and active, often with formal voting power, and almost always with the right to speak

---

[3] The growth of disciplines has created yet another kind of strain—a kind of "conflict of generations." Many older scholars are persuaded that not merely more, but different *kinds* of people, are being recruited to their fields, with different motivations, life styles, work habits, aspirations, and conceptions of the subject. Several respondents said that they would not have been attracted to the field as it now is. The transformation of these disciplines, in both size and character, create very deep tensions between older and younger faculty members, and between faculty and students.

and not merely observe. There may be good reasons why this move toward "participatory democracy" in universities is necessary or desirable, and the strength of those arguments surely varies for different kinds of decisions and in different kinds of institutions. But whether or not the presence of students on committees improves the *quality* of decisions, it is certain that they enormously increase the time and energy needed to arrive at decisions. Decisions that formerly were made by a dean or department chairman or a few like-minded senior professors are increasingly being made by larger heterogeneous groups of faculty and students, and are the outcome of lengthy discussions and negotiations. The elaboration of the formal and informal machinery of university government toward greater "participatory democracy" is greatly increasing the demands on the time and attention of the ordinary faculty member.[4] The transformation of much university government from *administration* into intramural *politics* creates another and highly distracting set of demands, which elsewhere has begun to seriously interfere with the intellectual and professional activities of academic men.

In addition, there are tensions arising out of growing resistance to the war in Vietnam, and increasing hostility to war-related research. A great deal of the research done at universities in recent years has been supported by the Department of Defense, and many people at leading uni-

---

[4] The number and frequency of faculty meetings at M.I.T. have more than doubled over the past five years.

versities want to shift the emphasis of research efforts toward America's very great domestic problems of health, welfare, and protection of the environment. Some demand that the universities end all of their involvement with military research immediately. While a commitment to change in these respects is shared quite widely, activist students tend to be more radical in their demands than the faculty as a whole. And this basically political issue is a new but growing source of tension between some students and their teachers.

In addition, increasing numbers of students (and they include some of the ablest) are expressing doubts about the moral basis and consequences of scholarly research. Such students argue that when a society and/or its government is corrupt and repressive, as in their view ours is, then any increase in knowledge or technical capabilities must strengthen these evil powers against those who struggle to replace the "system" by a more humane and beneficent one. The logic of such a position would seem to lead to withdrawing from scholarly work altogether. But many students hold or sympathize with such views without being prepared to make a life decision on the basis of them. Nevertheless, such views inevitably affect their attitudes toward their studies and their professors, and this creates the most difficult, if subtle, tensions between themselves and the faculty. These views are in a sense more corrosive of the student-faculty relationship than are "political" differences, since they strike at the central values and assumptions of scholarship, and thus are the most basic kinds of rejections that teachers could experience from their students. These views are an emerging force in American universities.

These emerging problems may have a cumulative effect on life in a major university that is greater than those detailed in the earlier parts of this chapter. They have led some academic men to question the viability of the university as it is presently constituted, and to begin to speculate on what alternative forms of organization of "higher education" might be imagined or invented. It is clearly too early to write an obituary of the American university; it has great resources and an inherent flexibility which may allow it to find ways of dealing with new as well as old strains and tensions. But the process of rapid large-scale change—whatever the outcome for the university—inevitably involves stressful conditions, and these in turn disrupt in a number of ways the day-to-day relations between members of the faculty and between faculty and students.

4

LABS
AND LAWNS

The students and faculty members discussed in Chapters 2 and 3 came from the same school. To carry the discussion a step further, I will compare M.I.T with a college which differed dramatically in its physical, social, and psychological setting. While the interplay between the formal and hidden curricula will continue to be a significant theme, the focus will be on certain assumptions that in the past underlay the education at these schools. I will suggest some of the ways in which these assumptions determined the questions that were raised about each school's effectiveness and its influence on what students learned both in and out of the classroom. The descriptions of these two campuses are how they looked to this observer a decade ago. Both schools have changed and continue to change in many significant ways. Both now hold less tightly to their own model of the "best student." Each of their conceptions of education shows a trend toward more diversity than in the past, and there is more flexibility in the ways their students now can achieve that education.

LABS AND LAWNS

Wellesley is a liberal arts college for slightly less than two thousand women, where intellectualism and concern for the students' moral and personal development go hand in hand. The campus has gently rolling lawns and well-pruned trees. At the time that I knew it, most of the buildings were American Gothic. The college setting appeared to exert a strong pull on the lives of most of the faculty. Their aspirations, their delights, their frustrations all seemed bound up in the life of the college and in the lives of their students. Faculty members had invested deeply in their students and their education. Their expectations for the student included both academic and character development.

The language that faculty members used in discussing students drew heavily on agricultural images. One task of education was "cultivation." This meant supplying students with the proper nutrients in order to promote firm, straight intellectual and emotional growth. A student up for disciplinary review was described as a "bad seed." There was a strong consensus that another task of the college was to provide continuity between the past and the future. Change was often spoken of as cyclical, not linear, and viewed as the recurrence of patterns over time. This shared attitude to time and change, extended and associated with the expected recurrence of patterns, seemed to this observer similar to the time sense found in agricultural societies. A number of the faculty spoke as though they saw their role as resembling that of gardeners nurturing young plants.

Not all the students, however, imagined themselves in quite this light. But it was clear that most of them assumed the attitudes and perspectives of their teachers, if they had not arrived already committed to them. There was a shared belief in the value of a liberal arts curriculum, particularly one which emphasized Emerson's "know thyself" injunction. Introspection was perceived by most members of the community—young and old—as a means to fuller self-realization. There was a concern for scholarship and proper attention to the demands of each discipline, be it English literature, history, or mathematics; but it was also considered proper that ethics, motivation, and the plight of the individual should be central parts of classroom discussions.

All this seemed straightforward and explicit enough; but there were related trends and some attitudes and responses shared by the campus community that were less directly stated. For example, students and faculty were almost always polite, and anger was unfailingy contained. Aggression tended to be directed inward upon the self rather than outward against others. Thus, when a student was confronted with an academic problem, she almost always looked at herself to see what was wrong. She may have mocked the college's image of the student as a plant that needed cultivating, but she reinforced it by accepting the notion that her failure implied that she was a "bad seed." She blamed her brain before blaming the college.

This last observation was borne out among the 10 percent of the students consulting the college psychiatrist. More than one-third of these students gave "depression" as the chief reason for coming in for interviews. Their sense of helplessness, with an associated drop in available psychic energy, was most often directly the result of the harsh judgments which they had made on themselves. This judgment was reinforced by their faculty and classmates. (There were striking exceptions to this among several faculty members and two deans, but their compassion stood out in marked contrast to the general trend.) High grades and proper behavior protected many students from the "sophomore slump," as it was called. Those few students with outstanding academic records who became depressed (primarily from a crushing perfectionism) evoked strong sympathy from the faculty, though often as not scorn, born of envy, from classmates.

Most of the students, majors in political science and in history, as well as young athletes, were quite consciously preparing themselves for a future role as wife and mother. They accepted the then current social definition of a woman's function but not without a certain confusion. This confusion was reinforced by the ambivalence of some faculty members, who would deprecate society's norms for women, while defensively exaggerating the importance of the intellect at the expense of feelings.

Eventually this ambivalence was carried forward by the students, particularly the most able academically, when they found themselves hiding their interest in intellectual competence. They were afraid, they said, that their intellectual abilities would interfere with developing and maintaining lasting, close relationships with men. These students pointed out that they were strongly supported in this feeling by several women professors. The strong currents of this conflict, however, did not surface directly but remained embedded in the hidden curriculum. The few adults who acknowledged the issue, who did speak openly about it, were exceptions to the rule.

Another, larger group felt that their worth as women derived from knowing some aspect of the culture in depth and serving as the carrier of this knowledge. They seemed to view themselves as providing both biological and social continuity between the generations. These students, like many of their faculty, spoke of time as extended where patterns could be expected to recur. Many students said explicitly that their function in life was to provide the continuity of tradition.

Those students who were trying to find a way to relate to men at the same time that they developed their interests in high energy physics or art history were genuinely involved in an expressive approach to their education. They were finding their own special voices. Ironically, they were usually perceived by their peers as fiercely instrumental, interested only in getting A's for graduate school and in winning the post-graduate fellowship. It was the critical students themselves who were seen as the expressive members of the community, not only by most of the faculty but also by the majority of their peers. On a closer look, however, it was the latter group of students who were "playing the game," achieving the rewards of a Harvard Law School husband and securing their place in suburbia by their attention to that other curriculum. Expressive and instrumental involvements in education are relative concepts, as we will see even more sharply at M.I.T.

The pattern of instrumentalism appeared at first look to be more obvious at M.I.T., though its actual effect on the students was less readily discernible than would seem to be the case. A decade ago the corridors and stairwells gave testimony to their usefulness. They were long and straight, many with pipes exposed overhead, and all painted a drab gray-green. (Now deep blue or orange, set against white, has recently begun to replace the green.) The campus itself was laid out at the turn of the century in geometric patterns with large utilitarian Roman temples interspersed with square or rectangular patches of lawn. Ten years ago the grass was gradually being taken over by expanding parking lots and new laboratories. (Now the buildings are interspersed with small gardens, islands in the sun.)

Here research and academic achievement were and

THE HIDDEN CURRICULUM

still are linked, often directly, to subsequent success in the society outside the university. Ten years ago, as now, the Institute selected one applicant out of four (almost the same proportion as Wellesley). The students' College Board scores ranked nationally in the upper 5 percent. Eighty percent of the graduating class moved on to some further graduate education.

It was not particularly surprising to find that the faculty frequently used the image of the machine rather than that of the plant when discussing students. A department head was concerned with making a "good product," a freshman adviser spoke of the "pressure" making some students study "mechanically, without thinking." "Students are so keyed up under pressure it takes them weeks to decompress."

The imagery of the machine reflected an easy, frank self-appraisal. If something that one was doing was ineffective, then it was important to know what was wrong and "apply a correction factor" in order to get results. This pragmatic position contrasted with the sometimes crushing sense of personal failure (the "bad seed" again) and helplessness associated with the agricultural image at Wellesley. Even more pervasive than the machine image, the ethic of hard work was (and is) the vital means for becoming the highly competent expert in science and, even more so, in engineering. "Hard work," in the words of a perceptive dean, "is the way to salvation."

Students with academic problems characteristically first

LABS AND LAWNS

looked outside themselves to find out what was wrong. Was the professor making unreasonable demands? Was the course disorganized or the exam tricky? Was the unknown element in the chemistry laboratory contaminated? Many students then added: Did I work hard enough?

While there were obvious differences between the theoretical physicist and the civil engineer, they shared common notions of cause and effect and a predilection for operational definitions. They seemed practical, even somewhat hardnosed, when compared with the liberal arts faculty with its Platonic, traditionally oriented definitions. Faculty and students at M.I.T. asked, "How well does it work?" Many added, "Why does it work?" The philosophy of the gardener was in contrast to the perspective of the toolmaker. The aims, aspirations, and indices for measuring achievement were radically different in the two settings. The words that most captured this difference were —in the college, *nurturance,* and at M.I.T., *competition.*

The basis for the students' feeling good about themselves at the two schools became linked to the prevailing norms in each environment. At M.I.T. ten years ago (this, too, has altered somewhat in recent years), approximately 10 percent of the students sought out the psychiatrist during their time in college. Their visits were described with such phrases as "I need a tune-up." Others wanted to "retool," "add gas," "get the carburetor adjusted." Depression, as at Wellesley, was the most frequent presenting problem, but it arose from a different source. Instead of harsh self-judgments, it had its origins in high expectations, sometimes beyond reach. The students' helplessness came from the extreme gap between what they were and what they wanted to be. They saw no immediate means to achieve their ends and did not seriously consider lowering their sights or re-evaluating their aims. Since one of the consequences of depression (from whatever cause) is a reduction in the energy available to the individual, the depressed student at M.I.T. had a diminished capacity for hard work; and this, in turn, cut off one of the principal means of "salvation," for feeling good about oneself again.

Anger was openly expressed and directed outward, not inward upon the self—though not to the extent of ignoring thoughtfulness and regard for social decency. But in the matter of student pranks, these students showed a degree of sophistication, imagination, and certainly aggression which far exceeded that expressed by students at Wellesley. There was the time some years ago, and already part of the mythology, when students quickly soldered a trolley car to the tracks during its brief stop to pick up passengers in front of M.I.T.

The hidden curriculum at these two schools included assumptions about the male and female roles that were derived from a particular culture at a specific time. Some of the difference may have reflected the male versus the female role. It is clear that the students, whether men or women, faced very different sanctions on the expression of aggression, on the implicit models of "good student" at each institution. The students at these two schools, whether men or women, faced very different sanctions in many areas other than that of sexual behavior. These differences could be seen in the accepted modes for the expression of aggression and even in the characteristic cognitive styles at each institution. Every school has a cluster of adaptive patterns associated with academic success. (The students were more likely to achieve high grades with intellectualization at Wellesley, and with selective negligence at M.I.T.) Because the hidden curriculum encourages certain solutions to educational and personal problems, because it provides one type of encounter and not another between students and faculty at a particular school, it has a significant influence on the students' adaptive response to their education. This relationship between adaptive pattern, cognitive style, and the ultimate use students make of their education is what underlies the importance of the hidden curriculum at any school. A careful examination of a school's hidden curriculum can often reveal whether its students use their education or are used by it.

How, then, do colleges and universities commonly judge their effectiveness, their impact on their students? They have a series of assumptions which become the basis for their decisions about their own effectiveness rather than actual feedback, raw data, from which to make these inferences. Many of the assumptions relate to norms and standards; some professors are aware of them; for others they become part of the given. Some of these standards relate to the incoming students. In certain schools they are selected on the basis of high College Board scores, superior vocabularies, and proof that they know particular kinds of facts. Moreover, the scores indicate that the students are capable of solving a specific class of problems, that they can give the right answers under the press of time. It is precisely these skills which are relevant for survival in today's colleges and universities, certainly in the elite schools like the two just discussed.

Colleges judge themselves on the number of their graduates who go on for higher degrees. They do not collect statistics on the divorce rate of their graduates, or the contributions to a discipline of those who did not receive the Nobel prize. Implicit are the notions of merit, professionalism, expertise. More recently colleges have compared the academic and research credentials of their faculty: publications, prestige, scholarly reputation. The American Council on Education, for example, has recently ranked universities and academic departments by drawing heavily on these criteria for its judgments.

These generally are the standards that faculties apply, their assumptions being that this is the best, if not the only, way to ensure continued excellence of higher education. The college administration finds and recruits the students who test out as the brightest in the country, and a faculty is selected on the basis of scholarly merit—that is, research and publication. A prestigious faculty helps create an intellectual climate which attracts the best students and keeps them intellectually engaged.

Certainly there have been some modifications of this. A number of academicians have urged that the criteria be broadened to include professors whose first commitment is to teaching students, with research and publication playing a secondary role. And with the expansion of black enrollments to include many black students who do not achieve high exam scores, there have been changes in admissions policy. But these are peripheral changes; they do not alter the present pattern but are exceptions to it.

These are oversimplified observations on how colleges and universities evaluate themselves and on the ways that professors and universities function. I do not mean here to judge the worth of the assumptions or the criteria, nor to find flaws in the argument, but rather to see what the effects of such criteria are. Do they work? What effect do they have on students and on the learning process? What do they leave out that should be taken into account? (They may well serve as rationalizations for maintaining the hidden curriculum!)

From these data the university learns very little about the degree or nature of a student's involvement in his own education. But the focus on grade scores and graduate training does tell the student where the university places its emphasis. His rank on college entrance exams and his grades in comparison with those of his classmates all reinforce the student's judging of both his future competence and his present sense of worth.

Moreover, rank in class or degree level tells the faculty and the university almost nothing about the ties that bind their students to their education—whether these ties are guilt, delight in mastery, or passive ingestion of all that is fed to them. The grade, of course, does in part reflect the student's capacity to regurgitate what he has been fed or may be positively correlated with the intensity of his guilt. Grades that serve as rewards are no basis for judgment of students' commitment or their capacity to explore. However, the tasks of the hidden curriculum do engage the student's attention in large measure because the mastery of those tasks is so closely linked to the formal grade. But the grade, by itself, will not tell the professor about the immediate impact of his formal curriculum on the way his student "connects" with that curriculum—whether he develops an instrumental or an expressive approach to those tasks of the hidden curriculum.

The hidden curriculum imparts to the students what particular performance is wanted from them. It signals to them that an instrumental or an expressive approach pays off, that the university or college is in reality interested in what he or she has been or is, not in what he or she could become. The university is actually concerned with hedging bets, taking a safe course with minimal risks. Why should the student be expected to do otherwise?

This may be a general problem of a mass system of education. By the nature of its size, and by the assumptions upon which it rests, a mass system generates an instrumental-reward structure which inhibits exploration of the margins of a field, the taking of informed intellectual risks. The college degree is an admission card into a highly competitive society. It has both work and class benefits attached to it. Without plan or formal faculty approval, instrumental rewards (and approaches to learning) have become the focal point of higher education. One sees it perhaps most clearly in elite professional schools of law, medicine, and engineering, but it is not absent in leading liberal arts universities and colleges. As I have already written, students are screened carefully before admission; high academic performance is the measurement that everyone learns to respect, for it leads to the right fellowships, the right jobs after school. (The "high risk" type of admission is precisely that, and such students almost always know that they are exceptions to the rule.) High grades often conflict with some of the student's legitimate strivings in late adolescence and early adulthood; they inhibit and constrain his ability to explore and to be open to new encounters. Most universities and faculties want their students to be able to have a variety of encounters, to learn from taking some intellectual risks, but the process by which they educate their students often creates circumstances which are destructive for many and inhibits any approach other than gamesmanship.

Students are part of a dynamic and very complicated

system; thus their failure or distress becomes the university's failure and distress. The difficulty is that such failure may not become apparent until a generation has passed. Those students who resolve the difference between the two curricula by simply denying that such differences exist may well have a comfortable passage through college. They have conformed to an accepted—in fact, an expected—pattern. And by denying the existence of dissonance within the college, and beyond that within the larger society, they have a far easier, more comfortable time of it. But the student who denies that dissonance exists usually runs the risk of being unable to change when he is confronted with new circumstances. We see this manifested years later in men from all disciplines holding onto past methods, forms, attitudes, even after these have proved obsolete. At universities there is a conflict between graduate students and those professors who adhere to a set of procedures and requirements which no longer serve an educational purpose.

Judging the student's strategies and ploys in response to the hidden curriculum, then, is not an easy matter. What yardstick can be applied? For example, those strategies that give students the highest short-term payoff do not necessarily serve them well in the future. They may master both the formal and the hidden tasks on campus, but the price may well be an exacting one: a narrowing of experience; limited access to learning; overspecialization (whether as revolutionary or as economist). In terms of performance and immediate success, the rewards are theirs, but neither learning nor growth has necessarily been advanced. For what has become required of students today does not automatically further their knowledge of chemistry or architecture or sociology. Nor does it further their psychological development or prepare them for the world they will be living in twenty years after graduation. Indeed, both the social circumstances that shape their lives and the specific tasks with which they are confronted will be profoundly different from those in the two curricula they encounter today. Their principal adaptive responses will then be considerably different from the present ones.

Their cognitive style and frame of reference differ, often dramatically, from those of students who hear the dissonance and try to understand it. These others are often excited (and occasionally disturbed) by its presence and are frequently moved to some action directed at reducing its level. This may result in some form of political action; a civil rights commitment; or, in another direction, in withdrawal, alienation, or the kind of cynical gamesmanship in which students scoff at any commitment save to serve their own immediate ends. (They successfully manipulate their classmates, professors, and dates without the constraint that comes from caring.) It is not a matter of campaigners for Senator McCarthy or drug freaks or fraternity men. Examples of all types of student responses—those who naively deny the dissonance on campus, those who are disturbed and moved to commitment by it, those who use it cynically to manipulate the community, to cite three —can be found among all groups, from Black Power advocates, to those on the New Left, to members of Young Americans for Freedom. The politics may differ, but the means the students adopt for achieving their ends are often the same.

Educators are largely innocent of the student's strategies and ploys. They seldom know whether their students are manipulating their environment (and their tutors) or whether they singly and successfully deny conflict and screen out issues which obstruct successful academic performance. What in the college environment contributes to the making of a student radical or a dedicated scholar? The answers to this question depend on one's perspective, on one's long-range hopes for the student and for the society. If the yardstick for measurement is academic standing or niceness of fit to immediate academic or social demands, then the measuring process is a relatively simple one. If it is emotional and intellectual growth and ability to move with the times, one must make quite a different judgment. This measuring process is far more complex than the first; all cause-and-effect relationships have become conditional. But few educational enterprises have sufficient concern for the future adaptation of students. The hidden curriculum suggests that they are far more instrumental in their approach to education than one might suspect by looking at the formal curriculum. They have gone to considerable lengths to select students who will succeed within the terms the academy has already defined. Those who cannot adjust, who permit extraneous, often emotional, issues to intervene, may be accepted into the college community (in some instances assigned a favorable status as the sensitive, alienated young man or woman), but they are not the university's more successful products.

Those who have problems—studying, adjusting, growing up, etc.—are provided with help from the counseling or psychiatric service. It is a civilized approach to survival of the fittest, with sympathy and understanding and even a second chance offered to those who find it difficult to cope. The students can drop out, travel, work, pass a year or two "growing up," and then return. What is often omitted, though, from the academic environment is a prime function of education: the learning of how the individual can express his uniqueness and still survive within his environment.

Knowledge of this relationship between development and experience is essential if the faculty are to understand how students integrate their lives at college with their past. This is really not as formidable an injunction as it sounds. Professors do not have to function as psychiatrists or abandon academic standards of excellence and rigor in an effort to reach the student. But they must recognize the student's perspective and perceive where and how the university cuts into both their own and the student's life space. It is to the student's sense of reality that they are largely blind, even when they are most compassionate.

The college experience, however, often seems to filter out the student's past, to reshape it until it fits the faculty's conception. The extent to which the college experience is preparing the student for some future, often quite unanticipated, role in later life is often unexamined, unacknowledged. The reality is glossed over by myths about the student's future.

In the light of the conditions facing our culture—the rapid rate of change, the danger of obsolescence or, even worse, extinction—any educational experience, whatever else it does, must increase the student's capacity to deal honestly and directly with conflicting evidence. The survival of the university depends on rapid, reliable feedback between faculty and students on the complex social, psychological, and technical problems of higher education. Students and faculty members who respond to ambiguity with innocence or denial often come to define their individual worth by how well they adjust, how comfortable they feel in relation to their immediate surroundings. They may have achieved that comfort by completely blocking out the contradiction between the two curricula. The danger of such comfort is that it closes off the need for feedback, shuts out the dissonances that resound in our fast-changing universities and society. All participants must recognize their own unique and special voices while learning to listen to the dissonance around them.

The separation of the formal and hidden curricula in the minds of the faculty creates another set of problems.

In the effort to reduce the noise and the conflicts around them, professors often misread the cues which their students signal, and rely on images of nurturance or the ethic of hard work. They do not observe a student's anxiety, or realize that a connection is being made between distrust and learning, or grasp that a student is avoiding the kinds of intellectual risks and discoveries which the professor wishes his class to undertake. Indeed, many faculty members, in their eagerness to get on with their own work, resort to the same kinds of denial or belief in a local mythology as do some of their students. Their lectures contain the necessary information; there is little recognition of the inevitable fall-off of attendance as the weeks progress, or of the passive response of the majority of the class. Or, if acknowledgment is made, it is soon wrapped in the comfortable assertion that students are free agents, they can attend lectures, take advantage of the library and the faculty as they see fit, cull through a bibliography, learn on their own. The professor, after all, is neither qualified to function as a guidance counselor-analyst nor paid to fulfill that role. The proof of the students' success or failure is found in the exams which test how much information students have absorbed and can accurately play back.

This faculty response tends to enhance the student's sense of alienation; it is confirmation of his suspicion that no one up there is listening. Further, such a separation made by the faculty often creates a similar separation in the student's mind, with consequences that appear to lead to a gap between public and private, overt and latent, ways of perceiving the world. Placing them in well-insulated boxes, he hazards developing a life style in which long-term consequences are ignored and only narrow and limited attention is paid to complexity.

One means of countering the tendency to separate the two curricula is to ensure affect, even delight, in the encounter of the student with the content of his course (and with his professor at least some of the time) *at the same time* that he gains intellectual skills. Neither the removal of all restraints nor the absence of pleasure in learning is an appropriate paradigm.

So many students in colleges and universities develop competences without affect or delight. They get their rewards from grades on papers they have written and not from the excitement of working through the idea in the paper. Their world is often closed to pleasure in academic pursuits. They humorlessly or angrily pursue their short-term goals of turning in assignments or "destroying the university." Twenty years later such students are vulnerable, with their narrow range of supports for their self-esteem. Their brittleness may well persist, since they are dependent on society's equivalent of grades. The social scientist of a generation hence may study his subject in order to satisfy his abstract curiosity about a problem of relevance to his field and be indifferent to the individuals he has studied. The questions which such a social scientist poses are likely to be influenced by the absence of concern for his subject as individuals. The presence of a few such scholars poses little threat; but should society sanction such encounters between the researcher and his "data," we would already be living in a very different, less humane, far more instrumental world.

Many in higher education disagree with this approach, contending that we should concentrate on training the mind. But those who hold this view are cutting themselves off from important information about themselves and their influence on their students' education. They ignore the hidden curriculum at considerable cost. Only in recent years have we seen what the price of a simplistic model can be for the education of students, for the security of faculty and administrators, and indeed for the life of the university itself.

One professor of science decided to shift some of his energies from research to teaching. He determined to spend six or more hours before each lecture thinking through the most coherent, comprehensible presentation of each morning's subject. The lectures were brilliant, delivered without notes and with great elegance. But many students were put off. They felt diminished by the man's brilliance—not grateful at all for his thoughtfulness. "How can I ever see this subject with such clarity, such assurance? I might as well give up aspiring to the top of that field." They knew nothing of his struggle before each lecture to achieve the very clarity that put them down.

Not only is it likely to be impossible to remove the discrepancies between curricula, but it may even be undesirable, since it would involve an unnerving degree of social programing and manipulation of reward structures, which could not and should not be done. We can learn by listening carefully to the mixed messages, and from this experience, in large measure, will come the continued excitement of education.

5

EDUCATION FOR COMPLEXITY

> *It's a different situation now in that almost all I do, the expectation of me is to apply creatively things that I have learned. In the undergraduate situation you are still in the process of doing the learning rather than trying to apply it creatively. The kind of reinforcement that I got from being successful as an undergraduate does me little good here. It doesn't convince me that I can do Ph.D.-caliber creative research. This is something that you have to find out all over again on the Ph.D. level. Your successes in high school, in college may convince you that you can do useful work. You may be just a great learning machine, not able to do constructive research.*
> —A Graduate Student

A third-year undergraduate student in the study referred to in Chapter 2 came in to me for his research interview a week after John F. Kennedy's assassination. He had been discussing a laboratory project with one of his professors when a secretary broke in and said that Kennedy had been shot. They talked about it rationally for a few minutes before returning to their previous discussion. Two days later, while watching the funeral on TV, the student saw videotape replays of people on the streets of New York bursting into tears when they first heard the news of Kennedy's death. He was startled by the contrast of his own and his professor's initial controlled efforts to take in the death with the uncontrolled emotional reactions of the "outside world." He began to cry and left the TV room to hide his tears from his classmates. He asked me in the interview whether the academic world concentrated so much on the brain that it ignored the heart. Did he risk losing his ability to feel, to cry, to feel compassion?

Major political and social events of the past decade (the war in Southeast Asia, the assassination of a President, the black revolt) have had a direct impact on the hidden curriculum. In the early 1960's about one-quarter of college men took off a semester or more before returning to school to complete their degrees. As the war escalated and draft calls rose, the number of such students leaving school dropped dramatically and academic survival took on another meaning. When the deferments of graduate students were sharply curtailed several years ago, there followed an immediate 100 percent increase among students applying for draft-deferred admission to medical schools.

A profound, though indirect, effect of these events has been on the growing sense of psychological helplessness of many students. They feel less able to achieve their aspirations or bring about those conditions in which they can feel good about themselves. These events have diminished their sense of worth and thus their self-esteem.

EDUCATION FOR COMPLEXITY

The equation by which individuals build up and maintain their sense of worth includes those real and fantasied connections with the "leader," with large events. When the leader is dramatically removed or events suddenly shift, the model of the followers' world may be severely shaken. Then begins the search for another, often even simpler, world view. Many seek outside themselves for an explanation of their inner pain and sense of bereavement over the loss of the leader. They say: "If we can only get rid of permissiveness (or Communists, or the establishment, or capitalists, imperialists, etc.), then everything will be all right."

Another reaction to major social fluctuation is disillusionment.[1] A loss of faith in the previously ordered world further increases the sense of helplessness, and so often there follows a dehumanization of those who are thus affected. The long-term consequences of such disillusionment may well be apathy and further alienation. The individual may say: "I got burned once by caring. I'm not going to care anymore; I'm just going to cool it."

The many changes within the present generation have placed great strains on the institutional and interpersonal

[1] Alan Moorehead in *Darwin and the Beagle* (New York: Harper & Row; 1969), p. 169, describes Darwin's reaction to a severe earthquake which hit Valdivia on the south Chilean coast while he was ashore there on February 20, 1835. "A bad earthquake," Darwin reflected afterwards, "at once destroys the oldest associations; the world, the very emblem of all that is solid, had moved beneath our feet like a crust over a fluid; one second of time has created in the mind a strange idea of insecurity, which hours of reflection would not have produced."

processes for maintaining some continuity with the past. It is difficult enough at best to comprehend today's world. The loss of a major leader, the escalation of a near or far-off war, further strain the system and our ability to comprehend. Disillusionment, alienation, or cynical gamesmanship becomes the framework through which increasing numbers of students view their education. The specifics of the hidden curriculum may remain the same on a given campus, in spite of a war or a black revolt; the students, however, see its syllabus in a very different context from that of even half a decade ago.

Students receive one set of official, formal messages—the rules, the prescriptions, the goals. In effect, these are what one must do to pass, to succeed, to move ahead from university to the larger society. At the same time the students are monitoring another, more informal, covert set of cues that tell them what really matters—what in fact leads to rewards and success. It is a dissonance which affects those of us who have lived with it for some time. But it is one that permeates the life of all of us, though many of us choose not to hear it. And so its specific challenge—to San Francisco State no less than Harvard—is a general challenge to our entire culture.

The simplistic responses and judgments which are often made by the press, by the public, even by the faculty, are alarming. It is as though all of the history, the context, the complexity of life at a university did not exist, or at most, were irrelevant to the crisis at hand. So the furor over black studies is regarded simply as a function of the growth of militancy among black students on campus; the cry for coed dormitories is attributed to the sexual revolution, which in turn is attributed to widespread use of the Pill; and the battles over ROTC are just a plot hatched by SDS and left-wing agitators on campus who want to bring the university to a halt.

All of these causal explanations may contain a piece of the "truth"; they are also distortions of what is actually occurring, and as such, are dangerously misleading. For instance, many black students *are* militant and are certainly on campus in greater numbers than they have been in the past. Their demands represent a challenge to a view and, more crucial, a process of education that is held by many students and even more by professors and administrators on campus today. For a large number of black students, the gap between the rhetoric of change and the actual movement in their curriculum and in their lives is infuriating. Matters are not made any easier for them when they return home, many to the ghetto, during school vacations and discover that for all of their militancy, all of their commitment to their own roots, they have been affected by the college experience, have become estranged from family and neighborhood friends.

It is very easy to be misunderstood when writing about black students in higher education. I deal here with only one small fragment of this serious issue—the imperviousness of the hidden curriculum to change. In the past few

THE HIDDEN CURRICULUM

years, black high school students have been recruited to previously white institutions in increasing numbers. Many white faculty members and administrators—and white students—speak as though they saw themselves as going out of their way to make their formal curriculum far more available to blacks than in the past. This act has amplified (not increased!) the dissonance between the formal and hidden curricula.

A black high school senior applied for and received a $4,000 scholarship to a leading university. His large family's income for the same period was $3,800. He accepted the scholarship knowing that, by doing so, in a real sense it reduced his family's resources. He expected that college would help him deal more effectively with specific and general problems of the urban poor. He was angry when he found that most of his time had to be spent in sharpening his skill in answering problem sets in math and writing papers for political science in order to get a sufficient grade to hold the scholarship another year. His academic background had been "deficient," he was told by a teaching assistant. Having come from a school which served a custodial rather than an educational function (a problem not limited to black students), he lacked those skills needed for A's in the hidden curriculum of the white middle class. The message that he drew from his first year's encounter with higher education was: "Behave—put off your anger, your desire to change the ghetto for at least four more years. We'll pay you well to do it our way."

Another black freshman tried hard to swallow his loneliness, suspicion, and distrust. The cheery optimism of his white dean and his affluent roommate intimidated him. To acknowledge his suspicion of them, he felt, would be a sign of his weakness, not theirs, and would open him to further exploitation. Their denial of his anxiety led this freshman to the verge of rejecting the formal curriculum because he took it seriously and literally, in marked contrast to his classmates. He had not had sufficient time to learn that his classmates already knew about the hidden curriculum and secured their A's by playing their special game. His other choice, as he saw it, was to reject the assumptions which he inferred underlay his course of studies. So he settled on a political solution—black studies—where his judgment of "relevance" would be rewarded with the white man's grade. He was surprised at his white professor's defensiveness and self-righteousness. "No student can do this to me. How can he doubt my fairness in grading?" said his liberal professor. The student's demands for a black studies program was not understood by his professors to mean "Take me seriously. I feel deeply about this issue. Listen to me."

Many black students have been admitted to major universities without experience equivalent to white students in basic mathematics or the writing of term papers. The help offered these students, usually in the form of special tutoring, may have been both patronizing and unspecific to their needs, and thus become a further put-down. Much of this tutoring was superficial, not addressed to the specific skills the students needed to develop to master the tasks of the hidden or the formal curriculum. The failure to honestly engage these students has been compounded as they have sought political rather than educational solutions to their very real dilemma. This is most evident where the faculty or the administrators have responded in political terms and ignored the longer-term educational goals. This does not imply that political means cannot be used to serve educational ends. It does indicate, however, that colleges must examine with care and full participation of the students involved those aspects of the hidden curriculum which interfere with the learning of students, white or black.

Many educational experiments, not only those involving black students, have run aground on the hidden curriculum. The lesson to be learned is that experiments developed on campus to reform some particular excess or deficiency, often only partly understood, often fail. They may increase rather than reduce the dissonance because they fail to deal with the actual educational tasks assigned and rely on the rhetoric of the formal curriculum alone.

I do not mean to say that the blacks are either right or wrong in demanding black studies programs, but rather that all of these issues are complex—far more complex than is acknowledged by political militants or advocates of an academic laissez-faire position. To perceive and understand these issues requires a close look at the university, at the students, at the professors, and at the transformations that have taken place and continue to occur in all our lives. Conflicts on campus are intertwined with those of the larger society. The pace of change is far more rapid than most of us can acknowledge. The point sounds simple though its implications are complex: when we look at conflict on college campuses we need to consider the progressions within the society, within the university, and finally within the stages of development of the students themselves.

In the university, for example, there are changes in the role of the faculty: they have gained more prestige, more influence in certain instances; in some cases they advise political and economic decision-makers. The university's deans have been forced to consider whether or not to drop their responsibility of serving *in loco parentis* for students. And the latter have changed sufficiently over the last decade so that both they and some university officials have begun to ponder which attitudes and norms it is now appropriate for a university to insist on, particularly in matters relating to the student's private life. Cries are heard in the press for a return to an earlier time when law, order, respect for authority were thought to prevail. The hidden curriculum of the 1920's, for example, should give these commentators pause.

One major difficulty is that the rates of change within our society, on our campuses, and finally in the lives of individuals are rarely the same, or even synchronized. Both perceptions and expectations about what is happening certainly differ between individuals and between groups; and value systems can increasingly be expected to be wildly out of line with one another. The university may adopt one view, the society a second, and the students a third. (Japan is an example of that outcome, with 80 percent of its students alienated and furious; faculty members, with little prestige and even lower pay, are also alienated. The academic degree is irrelevant to economic survival.) The students themselves can be expected to have distorted perceptions of the faculty, of their needs, their intentions, their bases of self-esteem. The dilemma is thus aggravated.

Because of the rapid rate of change, it has become far more difficult to judge the dissonances that exist, particularly if one only looks to past experiences within the university as referent points. No longer is past experience valid as the primary basis for judgment about the present, though that experience may be as recent as fifteen years ago.

Consensus about the facilitating myths and paradigms of university life (at its crudest, the acceptance of the faculty's right to define authoritative knowledge) has collapsed. In other words, expectations, and particularly expectations about processes within the university, are dissonant as a matter of fact. This dissonance is in significant degree caused by the changes which make common perception difficult. These changes involve profound matters of value, and they are hitting different people at different times.

In earlier times, the college population was considerably more limited, both as to numbers and as to social class. Indeed, until late into the nineteenth century, higher education had little explicit utilitarian value for its limited constituency. It was not for mass consumption. The lawyers, the engineers, and the scientists who helped shape the industrial revolution were not usually university graduates. Until 1850 the nation's supply of engineers came solely from Rensselaer Polytechnic Institute and West Point, where they followed a utilitarian curriculum. Most lawyers began as apprentices without a B.A., taking their exams after extended periods of apprenticeship which also enabled them to learn to think and behave like lawyers and to memorize the necessary treatises for the exams. The college reflected its religious (and English) origins in its curriculum—Latin, Greek, mathematics, moral philosophy. The curriculum was designed to create mental discipline (while the college acted as moral supervisor) for a society and a culture that was perceived as stable; establishing continuity with the past was not a fundamental issue for the nineteenth-century American educator.

The actual form of higher education consisted of lectures and recitation. Students memorized long passages and theories which they would deliver by rote on request. Not surprisingly, much of the curriculum seemed irrelevant to the students of the nineteenth century. They often protested and on occasion resorted to violence, in an effort to change their environment. The students saw their enemy as the faculty rather than boards of trustees and administrators. Indeed, it was sometimes the forceful and imaginative college president (Charles Eliot at Harvard, Andrew White at Cornell, Daniel Coit Gilman at Johns Hopkins) who pushed through innovations in curricula, who forced the colleges to break out of their settled ways.

The nineteenth century educators' approach to reform was to provide alternate forms of education, to set up graduate and professional schools, with many of the new professors trained in Germany. Harvard provided for an elective curriculum which could free the students from the closed system of courses that dated back to the seventeenth century. By the twentieth century the open, elective system had become the dominant pattern at both the old elite schools and the state and land-grant universities. Its excesses and its unanticipated consequences, a fiercely instrumental approach to education which led to trivialization of learning and vocationalism, served to characterize the problem that confronted higher education in America. In becoming more utilitarian, college education provided a form of upward social mobility in greater numbers for different groups in the society. Again, students rebelled against the increased utilitarianism, this time the change occurring in the student culture: fraternity life and athletics became highly significant parts of the college experience. There were more youths and less insistence that they become part of the labor market early in life; thus adolescence was prolonged. Professors were still part of the opposition, for they were set up as antipodes to the student culture. And where some of them reacted against popular mass education—Irving Babbitt and the New Humanists at Harvard, Robert Hutchins at Chicago, Scott Buchanan at St. John's—they seemed only to verify the popular view of academics as fifteenth-century scholars arguing about Plato and St. Thomas Aquinas.

In short, the imbalance between the felt needs of students and the prescriptions of the university is not a new phenomenon. What dominated the battles then, as now, was the difference in perception about the direction in which the society was moving and the relationship between the university, and those within it who held positions of power, and the society outside. Although Harvard ceased training most of its students for the ministry by 1800, it was sixty years before a new president could change the curriculum.

There are important differences as well as similarities. The modern university does not have the luxury of a long time lag. The pace of change has accelerated to the point where institutions, such as universities, which are charged with both maintaining continuity and sustaining innovation have become severely strained. The number of values, and the aspirations derived from them, that are genuinely shared between—or even among—the generations on or off campus have dramatically diminished. The occasions where various members of the academic community can even come to know, and appreciate, where their colleagues stand occur less frequently as our universities grow in size, increase in complexity, develop new technologies.

Today we live in a period of unprecedented technological change, where specific skills and competences developed over a lifetime can be rendered obsolete in a matter of months, weeks, or days. The life style which sustained the special skill is also subject to revision. The steam engine had almost a century of extensive use before the internal combustion engine replaced it. In the air, the jet engine has now largely replaced the internal combustion engine within only a quarter-century and itself is likely to be replaced within a decade by the rocket engine. These innovations affect not only modes of transportation but also production methods. The semiskilled worker on the assembly line, the engineer, and the physicist each has to develop new competences and judge his worth as an individual in different ways as a direct consequence of the changes. Similarly, technological change affects the faculty and the curriculum in engineering schools: what is taught to whom and by whom. This rate of change is no trivial matter for those who cling tenaciously to their professional expertise, even in the face of evidence that it has become outmoded. It is as true for psychiatrists as it is for engineers or teachers or students. Rapid changes—occurring within one generation—increase the risk that life styles developed over decades may become, if not a hindrance, at least irrelevant in mastering a new set of circumstances.

How are we to educate ourselves and our students to live with so much complexity and so rapid a rate of change? This is a special problem for universities, for it is here that such issues should be most clearly perceived, by both the present generation and the next. The protests that have been made at Berkeley, Columbia, and Harvard may reflect a partial failure of these institutions to develop means to deal with the disjunctions between their past and their students' expectations for the future. At a minimum (this is not a total explanation for unrest), it is clear that members of these institutions were dangerously out of touch with one another; there can have been almost no effective communication, for example, between teaching assistants and professors, between professors and students.

One consequence is the erosion in the trust that has, in the past, existed among most university members. Negotiation has supplanted dialogue as a major mode of communication, and positions on educational as well as social and political issues have become dramatically polarized. The distrust affects not only personal relationships but the climate for learning as well. A student's distrust of his professor may lead him to engage his professor in a clever game where his self-esteem is based on one-upmanship—not on learning what he doesn't know, but on showing off only what he has learned. Distrust conspires to work against the interests of students and professors alike. Even more serious than gamesmanship as a threat to education is a political solution to the distrust issue.

An economics professor, teaching a statistics class, conducted a brief but imaginative experiment. He arrived one morning with a large empty goldfish bowl and two elongated canisters. One canister was filled to the top with two hundred white marbles; the other held exactly half that number, but all of these were black. The idea was to demonstrate a point about randomness as a statistical concept.

For about ten minutes he discussed randomness, defining it, analyzing the theory that lay behind it, and explaining the relevance of the marbles to his intended experiment. First, he said, he would take the two canisters and empty all the marbles, black and white, into the goldfish bowl. Then, after the marbles had been mixed together, he would draw one, blindfolded and at random, from the bowl. After each draw he would return the marble, mix again, and make another try. Before each draw, the students were to predict which color would be drawn. He offered each student five cents for every correct guess.

He was dismayed by the results. Only one student, a mathematics major, seemed to have grasped the point; he predicted white for almost every draw, the statistically correct response. The majority had predicted white after a succession of black draws, and black after several white ones, following the amateur gambler's hunch rather than the statistician's law.

His dismay soon gave way to puzzlement. His demonstration had seemed like a good idea. Where had the concept become obscure? He asked the class to explain why they had answered as they did, given the earlier theoretical exposition which they seemed to have understood. Nearly everyone indicated that he had assumed some hidden design or trick on the professor's part and simply did not believe the drawing was a random one. The mathematician who had performed so well was no exception: "I wanted to be different from the others. When everyone called out white for three or four draws and then switched to black, I decided not to go along with the herd and so stayed with white." Even he had assumed that the problem was not as straightforward as it had appeared to be and played the experiment as though it were an exercise in game theory, not statistics. He had defined his game as beating his classmates, not solving the statistical problem.

Several explanations of the results of the experiment were offered by other professors. One came from an economist, a highly rational man with little regard for the social nexus surrounding the students. He contended that greater pains should have been taken to make the experimental rules explicit, that randomness as a concept had obviously not been described with sufficient clarity. In his effort to explain the results, he did not consider relevant the way in which students viewed their encounters with professors in the classroom.

A poet claimed that this was simply an instance of human nature asserting itself. These students had had twelve to fifteen years of experience in the academic game of pursuing grades, looking for the trick in the question. Why should anyone be surprised at the response? It was based on their perception of the academic experience; and, regardless of the professor's intention, it was not necessarily an inaccurate judgment on their part. They had learned to be on guard, to be suspicious, to distrust.

The psychological need to impose order on a random process and the need to place something that is new or ambiguous so that it conforms to experience is not limited to students. Everyone has a private set by which he derives personal meaning from the cues that he perceives. In the thirteenth century, accidents seldom occurred; they were the work of some outside force, incubi and succubi. Today there is a different set of explanations for random accidents; there are those who are certain they are caused by complexes and the death wish.

It appears that our minds are not much freer than the minds of our ancestors. We have merely changed our frames of reference. Increasing our students' abilities to respond effectively to unexpected cues should be a central concern of higher education. At a minimum, this means that students must become aware of their own frames of reference, of their own perceptual bias. This is a theme that underlies this book. That is its professional—perhaps its narrowest—focus. The hidden curriculum is the covert frame of reference by which students organize and simplify the complexity and ambiguity that *is* today's university.

This approach leads to larger, and more serious, questions about higher education. What level of the student's experience must the teacher understand in order to have an accurate explanation for the observed results of education? Is he making educational decisions based on knowledge or on rationalizations? Is he addressing himself to that part of his student's personality that is free to act and make a decision, or is he dealing only with some defensive fragment of his personality?

One point flows from these questions: they suggest that the college professor and the dean need to understand the impact that the university environment makes upon themselves and upon the student. It means that the encounters that take place among students and between faculty and students have to be understood if one is to assess the way the university operates, the reasons why students learn the things they do, in the way they do, the reasons why they derive pleasure from, or become disaffected by, their university experience.

Knowledge of this interface is essential in a university,

for it enlarges our perceptual field and enables us to respond to far more cues when we consider the student's life on campus. If the faculty members can consider their responses to their earlier academic experience, their perception of their own college environments and what it appears to be exacting from them, then it may be possible to change the quality of what occurs in the classroom. It becomes easier to recognize what is being learned, and why, in a statistics experiment like the one just described. A student or a professor may inquire in the middle of a lecture about the information which is being picked up by the class; why students are tuning out the professor; what is he actually communicating, and to whom. This information makes it possible to restructure a course or a curriculum, or an institution, to improve the amount and the quality of learning that takes place within it.

In reality this is far more than a modest change in process; it means that both students and faculty must take into account their immediate environment in class and the more extended environment of the institution through at least four years; it forces a qualitative change in the encounter. Learning and teaching take place in a different field and become different actions from those which are traditionally performed when viewed from this perspective. When faculty members narrow their frame—limit the cues to which they respond—they limit their students' perceptual set and constrict their students' curiosity about the sudden, "the random" event.

EDUCATION FOR COMPLEXITY

Recently some of these concerns have shifted to the political arena. For example, critics argue that what the educator and the student need is accurate information about the power structure within the university. Who talks to whom? Who knows what is going on? Who makes the decisions? The educational community needs this information in order to make intelligent, educational decisions.

Political solutions do not necessarily alter the distance between the formal requirements and the hidden curriculum within the university. The most militant students, black and white, and some of the professors, now perceive the university in political terms, where forces or interest groups bargain for power. For some students, the academic side of university life has already proved highly unsatisfactory or irrelevant; and so political action and political participation provide the only meaningful experience on campus; indeed, it has become their substitute for education. For still others, the political response has been an angry, rebellious act: the student will no longer function as the polite recipient. It is clear that such militancy encompasses only a small percentage of the student population. But it does touch a responsive chord in many others who are less militant, less rebellious and disaffected, but who nevertheless are disturbed by significant aspects of the educational experience and of the larger society as it is reflected in the university.

These are questions that students are raising, and the

danger is not that they are challenging the university in this way but rather that they and the university officials too often settle on a political solution and ignore its educational implications. Students are demanding a voice in policy decisions; they are asking the university to change the curriculum, to shift from lectures to seminars, to provide courses on contemporary issues, but they run a high risk of ignoring central pressures in the environment itself, on the interaction between student and professor and the norms of the university. A course in alienation will make learning no more or less meaningful than one in methodology in the social sciences. A major in black studies *in itself* will create no changes in the academic environment if the end result is to establish another department which will, in turn, train a new generation of professionals.

We must look very carefully at the disparity and confusion created by the signals that students and faculty pick up from both the formal curriculum and the university's hidden curriculum; and we must examine the ways in which students respond or adapt to the formal and informal demands that the university makes on them. For some it is rebellion, for others it is getting A's. What is important, of course, are the consequences of this adaptation for the emotional and intellectual growth of the students. That is the goal of most education—to facilitate and enhance such growth. But somehow the process that has evolved within the university often tends to restrict this goal, to work against its realization.

EDUCATION FOR COMPLEXITY

One result has been the politicization of academic life, the translating of educational concerns into political bargaining over curriculum reform, and political pressures for new experimental colleges established within the larger university complex. But unless they affect the *dissonances* that exist within the university, unless they get at the relationship between what is learned and how it is integrated or used by the student, the reforms and the politics will not sufficiently alter education in the American university; and the next generation will find it no easier to manage the complexities, the pressures, or the confusions that confront it than the present one.

6

THE
ECOLOGICAL TRAP

Lemmings provide a dramatic example of an ecological trap where a species has outstripped its means for managing to live in some proximate equilibrium with its environment. The lemming population increases geometrically under the frozen tundra of a peninsula; every three or four years, a point is reached at which there are just too many lemmings in the available space, and they start their race to the sea. According to Professor Edward Devey at Yale and others, the lemming seems to be running blindly from other lemmings, in adrenal shock from having to decide a hundred times a minute whether or not those other lemmings crowding in on him are friends or foes. The lemmings' ability to adapt has not kept pace with their changed circumstances. Thus, the lemmings are caught in an ecological trap set, at least in part, by themselves.

We know examples of other ecological traps: New England ponds or Lake Erie; even the Los Angeles freeway may be one. The point is the same. A present mode of

THE ECOLOGICAL TRAP

adaptation has become obsolete or dysfunctional; and, in time, the species becomes extinct because the balance with its environment is broken. Habitats and living conditions change, whether by increases in population or by the intervention of man or other external agencies. This upsets the equilibria and puts a strain on the organism involved. They can adapt (though there are limits), but they can also panic or, alternatively, ignore the strain. Both of these responses decrease the organism's ability to see his surroundings, and thus contribute further to the environmental strain.

Higher education may well be facing an analogous crisis. The way in which the universities deal with the mounting distraction will shape them two decades hence.

Sir Geoffrey Vickers, a most perceptive observer of the British and American social scene, draws on the ecological imagery and further extends the relevance of the metaphor. He speaks specifically of the effect of the rapid state of change on the institutions, with the consequence of increasing risk of obsolescence:

> The skills, the institutions, and the ideas of hunting tribes served their needs far longer than did those of agricultural peoples, because they did not generate the changes which would have made them obsolete. Even the agricultural epoch, those last three hundred generations, which spans the whole era of recorded time, gave birth to civilizations which deserve to be called stable over several centuries,

in that their skills, their institutions, their ideas did not change rapidly from one generation to another. We now seem to be approaching a point at which the changes generated within a single generation may render inept for the future the skills, the institutions, and the ideas which formed that generation's principal heritage. If this is true, it looks like an ecological trap, though the determinants of the trap are social and cultural rather than biological.[1]

If Vickers is correct, if the analogy with the lemmings has any force, then within higher education students and faculty will need to examine seriously their current assumptions about their activities and institutions and check them against the present reality. Our patterns of governance and our processes of education no longer rest on wide agreement among almost all participants about the nature of the enterprise. An approximate consensus on the goals of education in this country and on the means to those goals can no longer be assumed. Our fathers' values and assumptions are no longer self-evident to our sons. The loss of this consensus is a profoundly important social and psychological event. It is a symptom of the "changes generated within a single generation."

There are other effects of this altered circumstance: increasing polarization of positions and growing distrust—both leading to increasing strain on the "normal" channels of communication in the classroom and in the govern-

[1] Sir Geoffrey Vickers: *Value Systems and Social Process* (New York: Basic Books; 1968), p. 79.

ing committees of universities. The number of shared assumptions diminishes in an information vacuum where we are hard pressed to know which assumptions no longer hold. Even more than in the past, the hidden curriculum will become the area where these underlying issues will be played out; its "syllabus" will be first and most deeply affected.

Many educators equate adaptation with the niceness of fit of the student's adjustment to the educational scene. Many professors focus on the student's short-term accommodation to the series of external pressures of the formal curriculum and use a reinforcement feedback system—grades. (Of course, it is often the only feedback available when one has three hundred students in a class.) "Successful adjustment" is a normative judgment and views "successes" in terms of niceness of fit. Adaptation, on the other hand, refers to the means that individuals use to accommodate to or change their immediate environment. Whether the means are "good" or "bad" depends on one's definition of survival over time.

There are special problems in higher education, especially in a university which is both contributing to and profoundly affected by the very rapid growth of scientific and technological knowledge. For example, the working circumstances of an optical engineer have altered drastically within the last decade. Until recently a lens of any complexity was the product of months of trial-and-error calculations. A computer now makes these computations in a matter of seconds. The optical engineer who obtained this accuracy through long periods of tedium and hard work finds this talent far less necessary and possibly even irrelevant to the new tasks that now face him. It can be argued that his previously successful adaptation to tedium had become so much a part of his sense of competence as an optical engineer that he would be psychologically unable to shift his cognitive style to one more consistent with the new tasks.

Can the educational environment lock some or many or all students into a narrow and rigid adaptive response? Do students in the process of becoming highly competent in some academic discipline or in a profession increase the risk of a rigid response? Are there educational contexts that extend, rather than limit, the students' range of adaptive responses? Precisely the same questions can be asked of the faculty. In the complexity of this post-computer world, my answer to these questions is not to give up on competence. Man's survival rests in part on greater competence, not less. But we must be clear about those linkages, processes, and interactions between students and their surroundings which free or, alternatively, severely limit their adaptive potential while they are learning a skill or discipline.

This latter outcome, if or where it occurs, can be viewed as the ecological trap of today's higher education. A student who makes an immediate, successful adjustment, such as mastery of the skill or even a high grade-point average, may achieve the feat in a manner that limits the possibility of shifting his adaptive style. Ecological traps develop where such longer-term consequences have been ignored, though to know about or anticipate these consequences is not an easy matter. A student (as well as his professor) may become locked into one view of man and come to base his sense of worth on one way of formulating complex social problems. He may misread or fail to read the evidence that would suggest some error in his view.

To put the issue another way: in the very process of achieving a set of interrelated educational objectives, a number of students appear to develop both cognitive and adaptive styles which then become so fixed that their ability to cope with new tasks or with altered circumstances may be severely limited. This may be the price that has been paid by the student for a *parochial* or short-term success in education. Some very able students maintain their high grade-point averages by closing themselves off from other activities (consulting source books) and from feelings (curiosity; delighted derivation of formulae; excitement over the Lorenz transformation; writing poetry, etc.) which they consider irrelevant to the completion of what they have come to see as their immediate educational task—passing the next quiz or handing in tomorrow's problem set.

So this rapid rate of social and technological change has made visible a question that in the not-so-distant past we could largely ignore. We must come to understand what it takes intellectually and emotionally for students to complete the assigned tasks of the modern university. We must look beyond the formal curriculum to the hidden curriculum in order to determine which tasks are relevant to the students' survival. We should analyze the influence of the university on their adaptation, on their strategies for survival. Consideration must be given to the changes in their psychological defenses against anxiety (and even the shifts in what makes for the anxiety in the first place) that enable students to contend with the specific stresses of their education. The number and the kind of internal, psychological changes that students make in the process of becoming educated vary widely from individual to individual and, I strongly suspect, from groups on one campus to those on another. A given change in adaptive response will also vary in its relevance to the student's present "adjustment" to what he expects or hopes to become in his later life.

We have seen in Chapter 2 some of the ways in which a group of students based their sense of worth on a specific institution's judgment of them. These students were all responding to one school—and a school with its special stresses, a relatively circumscribed set of career goals. I have not tried to show that M.I.T. is like or different from other schools: rather that some picture, some knowledge of these adaptive patterns can help us understand the learning situation for students in any college. On many campuses the same teachers who claim they want creative students so burden them with busy work that they have almost no time left to explore the limits of their new-found competence or to test or extend its relevance to their reality. Distraction has been institutionalized for both faculty and students, and managing this distraction becomes the first assignment, a matter of sheer survival for both faculty and students.

This theme of institutionalized distraction was revealed by both faculty and students in interviews at one institution. However, it has been heard as a major theme at a number of colleges and universities which differed widely in their formal characteristics. The kinds of pressures represented by institutionalized distraction, generated in part in the society outside the university, come to exert a significant effect on the hidden curriculum and, in turn, on the formal curriculum. It is also a pressure that has a considerable influence on the life styles of faculties and students, on those forms of adaptive response which become sanctioned on each particular campus.

For example, students request increasingly more and more of their faculties' time and attention. Such students perceive that their education is less than it could or should be because of their too limited contact with the faculty. They often seek to initiate social activities to get to know their professors. They ask for smaller classes or tutorials. Ironically, the students' education may in fact be even more endangered by such requests unless the underlying problem of distraction is also dealt with. For without some alteration in the faculty's commitments of time and energy, the faculty, faced with still another encroachment, may rely even more on institutional processes to protect them. The lecture and the quiz conserve the professors' time while furthering (at least to some extent) the students' education. A program for the faculty to know their students better, without a change in the conditions that exist in most universities, is unlikely to gain more than a token response. Such requests are in fact yet another distraction. What would cause more frequent and meaningful encounters between faculty and students that would not be a distraction for the faculty?

The model of the tutorial, residential college has been transported across the Atlantic Ocean from Oxford and Cambridge. In England the nurturing, the "care" of young men by older men has been as much the source of self-esteem as scholarship for some faculty. We can rarely create the conditions of elite residential Oxbridge Colleges, but we do need to find ways for faculty and students to come together in learning situations where they both have a significant stake in the work at hand and in the outcome. Student employment in the professor's lab may result in such an opportunity. This notion can be extended to political science, sociology, urban planning, etc. Courses centering on real and pressing problems (pollution, voter registration, arms control, etc.), developed and even taught jointly by faculty and students, may provide another situation where students and faculty can have common purpose. The encounters must be regarded as legitimate by all participants.

Although the above applies primarily to the faculty, the students are also faced with institutionalized distraction. Both are prisoners in the same box; the students' descriptions of what it feels like to be inside often coincide with the faculties' accounts. Both feel forced to make the most efficient use of their time. The general emphasis on "efficient communication" often seems to lead students and faculty to ignore signals from each other that in a narrow, short-term sense have been defined as distracting. Ambiguous cues usually need careful attention to decode and then to understand; under pressure they may simply be shut out or become the only object of attention at the expense of any goal. We have already touched on some of these ambiguous cues—the mixed messages, the dissonance that underlies much of the hidden curriculum. The classic example is the professor who says "Be creative" and rewards rote memory. The closer people come together, the more essential it is to understand these cues in an interpersonal relationship. This particular response to distraction—reliance on simple, unambiguous cues—does pose a potential threat to education; it denies the inherent complexity of life.

Consider the potential appeal for a student when he is

told by a colleague (either faculty member or student) that he should ignore subtlety lest he be penalized or co-opted. The more simple and direct the appeal, the more it may serve to diminish distraction (the self-righteous certainty that so often accompanies such appeals becomes a further protection). The stage is then set for political solutions to the problems of education, in a setting where the effect of those solutions on the quality and kind of education will probably go unexamined, except by a few suspect social scientists.

Several years ago, when I was interviewing a number of students in one institution, some of these students described the university as cold and impersonal and then went on to say that they had stopped dating and avoided bull sessions because both were "distractions." They had become impersonal in order to "maximize" their time, as one student put it. So their response to the press of distraction was to become cold and impersonal themselves. They didn't perceive that the faculty were caught in the same trap and that they too became impersonal as a way of dealing with increased distraction.

There are implications for "successful adaptation" in the cognitive models and life styles that students and faculty develop in order to organize and comprehend their experience in higher education. This is particularly so since these models serve as both the students' and faculty's means for sorting out the signals from the noise around them. (Students who do not go to class are "lazy.") They use them to help deal with the dissonance on campus, to decode the mixed messages of faculty and student intent as expressed in the two curricula. These models, with their latent assumptions about how and why students learn or teachers teach, may be expressed covertly in long-range plans and judgments about higher education. The model becomes the basis for major educational programs, for the grading structure in most colleges. One professor put it succinctly: "The quiz tempers the student's mind."

The risk of obsolescence, however, is great. The individual who has tied his sense of worth to the "correctness" of his model may not be able to read unanticipated, new cues from his environment that would have signaled a change in his educational or social circumstances. Such an individual would have no inclination to know that both his "model" and the adaptive position that it suggested had become "out of phase."

There is a point at which a particular adjustment to a given set of environmental pressures may become irreversible. The adaptive pattern that has become fixed is less likely to be responsive to further changes in the environment. But the optical engineer's obsessional attention to detail and the dinosaur's weight and size, developed over a millennium to cope with a piece of earth and other dinosaurs, became their undoing when confronted with a change in the conditions for their survival.

Unlike lemmings, man is complex and able to survive extreme stress, at least for the short term. The stresses and the pressures in education are subtle and operate insidiously. Man may not know until too late that he has paid a high price for his immediate adjustment to these stresses. The pollution of the air leads to an increase in deaths from respiratory disease. Coal miners with silicosis and emphysema are a special and dramatic case of short-term, apparent adjustment with irreversible, often fatal, long-term consequences. The physician who gives the miner elixir of terpinhydrate for his cough has relieved the symptom of the lungs' reaction to inhaled irritants. Their effect on the lungs may not become clinically evident until years later. Attenuating the symptom has obscured temporarily the underlying pathological process.

To put this in an educational context, a counseling service may direct its efforts toward adjusting students to the local conditions, reassuring them, supporting them in their immediate distress, and fail to consider, like the miner's physician, the cost to the student, or to society a decade hence, of short-term fitting in.

One major gain from an ecological perspective lies in its emphasis on complexity, on the interdependence of man and his surroundings. The short- and long-term consequences of the actual or possible interactions between human beings and their environment become the focus of attention. Such a perspective highlights the specific accommodation made by a species (or an individual of that species) to the constraints, the limits imposed by its environment.

THE ECOLOGICAL TRAP

We have found repeatedly at M.I.T. that when a student's sense of his worth is based principally on those narrow ranges of criteria of performance that are used by the institution, two things follow. First, the student's adaptation appears to be less likely to change, even in the face of new and different environmental pressures. Second, the student also appears to be less aware of the consequences of having adjusted than are his classmates. To fit the real diversity of students we may not need to teach them differently, we may just need to grade them differently.

As part of the research,[2] two groups of students were selected on the basis of their scores on a psychological test given to them early in their freshman year. We were interested in seeing whether students with similar adaptive patterns had similar academic fates as they moved through the institution. One group were chosen because they were marked by a desire to seek out new, complex social and cognitive experiences. The other group's responses to the same items in the personality inventory suggested that they were careful, orderly, avoided ambiguity where they could, and appeared to take minimal risks. The group seeking new experiences lost three times as many students through withdrawal or disqualification as the non-risk-takers in the first year, with no significant

---

[2] B. R. Snyder: "The Education of Creative Science Students," *The Creative College Student: An Unmet Challenge*, P. Heist, ed. (San Francisco: Jossey-Bass, Inc.; 1968), pp. 56–70.

difference in subsequent years. Moreover, the grade average for these latter students was consistently higher, despite the fact that there was no statistically significant difference on the scholastic aptitude and achievement tests of the two groups on admission.

Over the four years about a third of the students from the risk-taking group left the institution. The restless curiosity which characterized them is a quality that many faculty members desire in students. So the institution wanted these students, admitted them, and saw many of them leave. Indeed, we have been suggesting that it unwittingly forced them out.

Some faculty members believed that the admissions procedure was lax since so many of this group failed or withdrew. The argument seemed to be that the institution should admit students who would survive, with the assumption that the environment could not or should not change. "Adaptation," in this context, means adjustment to both curricula, with successful completion of the formal quizzes and exams. Had the institution followed this course of action, it would have lost the opportunity to learn more about some of the major costs of its tightly scheduled, competitive first year, plus the personal cost to the failing students. More serious, it would have decided to select students to fit a potentially maladaptive program. It did not do this but instead undertook a major reform of the first-year curriculum, still in progress.

THE ECOLOGICAL TRAP

One professor in a science department restructured his recitation section of a required course in order to engage the more creative students in a dialogue and to free them from the possible tyranny of extensive assignments. He limited the number of students to twelve, instead of the usual twenty to twenty-four. They sat around a table in a comfortable room; the discussion, like the surroundings, was far less structured than in most such sections. But the attendance of the creative students dropped off, while their more conservative classmates came regularly throughout the semester. The professor felt that his experiment was, by and large, a failure. But since the absent students did well enough academically, only the professor was directly concerned about these students and his experiment.

This experiment was embedded in an intensely demanding curriculum. Many who cut class were simply responding to the pressure to produce in their other subjects. Blinding themselves to the syllabus and working by the clock did not come as naturally to the creative students; it took, as one student put it, "constant vigilance to keep up." He hoped that after graduation there would be time to pursue the intriguing questions that he had heard raised in his few appearances at the seminar. For the present he had to ignore the questions and the seminar in order to make the time to keep up his grades.

Institutional pressures deprived both professor and students of the dialogue that the design of the section was intended to sustain. Most of the students reported in some detail how hard they had worked. Several of the "dropouts" said they had missed a real engagement with the subject even though they had mastered its syllabus.

The language and the imagery used by many of the faculty in this department to explain their educational philosophy is relevant. A department paper described the acquisition of knowledge as a "linear function between native intelligence and work." That is, the harder one worked, the more one learned. This value held by both faculty members and students in one institution caused the failure of an experiment in a single course; this is perhaps the characteristic fate of piecemeal rather than structural reform in education.

At present our evidence is only suggestive, but many otherwise well-qualified students whose cognitive style is concrete appear to leave physics after their experience with relativity theory, perplexed and uncertain of what they have been dealing with. In the context of the university, they define themselves as second-rate. To simplify the choice, an institution must develop more careful preselection or must experiment with teaching methods and approaches that would enable these students to master the abstract cognitive style. To preselect "more carefully" for conformist behavior would foreclose a continuing engagement of at least some students with some faculty

THE ECOLOGICAL TRAP

members in a rewarding (and urgently needed) reassessment of the process of education, and indeed, of the discipline. It would also reduce the proportion of imaginative and reactive undergraduates in physics, with consequences for faculty morale and institutional status. We need to modify the environment to accommodate a wider diversity of students with a greater range of adaptive responses than in the past, or else we will be in a trap.

From the study of the movement of the students into and out of the various academic departments, I was struck with the way the departments functioned like a colony of living cells. Each department had its unique, semipermeable membrane which let in its own nutrients and filtered out its own "waste products." Thus, syllabus-free students tended to move out of a particular department and congregate in another which, at that time, was actively changing its curriculum and its image to be more attractive to the risk-takers. The waste product of one cell often became the nutrient for its neighbor. The internal environment provided by each department was not uniform, since each was attracting a slightly different group of students and developing quite different "end products."

Some characteristics of the institutional environment clearly touched all of the departments, though not in equal measure. Some departments functioned like ecological niches, others as a kind of reservoir or supplier of students to several of the departments with rapid rates of growth. There were two departments that screened certain kinds of students out of the Institute entirely. The risk-taker who found himself in one of these departments as a sophomore was more likely to experience a drop in grades, more likely to accept the department's definition of him as lacking intelligence or motivation and simply withdraw from the scene of battle. (Some of those students went on in related fields in other institutions to do very well indeed; some dropped out of higher education altogether and made little apparent use of their capability.)

The presence of filters, the interaction between departments which affect the students, exist in all educational institutions. The presence of the hidden filters can be identified by carefully examining the movement pattern and from this inferring the tensions and the dissonances that develop between the formal and the hidden curricula. We found that we had to investigate the manifest and latent tasks for each department in order to begin to understand those adaptive patterns and coping mechanisms which students had to develop in order to master these tasks.

Some examples may make this more concrete and may suggest similar situations on other campuses. Most of the departments had key subjects in the sophomore or junior year which were designed to "separate the sheep from the goats." A high grade in these subjects was necessary in order for the student to be taken seriously as a major in that field. In some departments the high grade appeared to reflect the student's ability to "think like a mathematician"; in others it was believed that the student who was bound to the syllabus, who had earned a high grade, and who organized his life and his approach to the course in question would do well throughout his career in that major.

Moore, the able science major of Chapter 2, recounted his experience with one of these key subjects in his junior year. He had begun to question seriously whether he wanted to continue through graduate school in the field. He wondered about his life ten years after the Ph.D. "I was afraid I would be busy filling in tables and carrying the decimal point to the fourth or fifth position." He did not talk about this shift in perspective with his professors, but it did lead him to approach the key subject in his major in a very different way from that in which he had studied before. He said he no longer worried about the quizzes and spent all of his time reading references and textbooks that were related to the subject. He wanted to develop a feeling for the complexity, the difficulty, and the uncertainty in the field in order to help him decide whether this was the field for him. His grades dropped precipitously throughout the term. A year before, this would have scared him; now he was at most mildly annoyed with what he felt to be the "irrelevance of quizzes." Fortunately for him, Moore said, the final examination was cast in general terms. He was thus able to make full use of the knowledge gained from his own reading. He did see it as ironic that he received an A for the term. He went on to his Ph.D. in the field. In this instance the institution was able to spring its trap and recognize, reward, and retain a freer and more creative student.

There were other factors in addition to key subjects, the quality of the quiz, and the grades that served as filters of the students: the size of the class, the actual demands of a given subject on the student's time, the nature of the discussion in recitation sections. Some students felt intense shame in exposing their "ignorance" to classmates in the give-and-take of recitations and only went to large lectures, where they could remain anonymous.

Academic departments probably sorted the students in a manner that was largely unintended. The non-risk-takers were differentially rewarded in certain departments from those who sought out risks; the former stayed on this path, their scholarships secure. The educational and adaptive issues come together when the student who avoids risks and plays it safe receives reassurance from frequent quizzes, while that other student feels constrained by them.

At M.I.T. ten years ago, the hidden curriculum shaped the students' patterns of coping and their images of themselves as students and as individuals. This shaping process was certainly not part of any overt plan. Before we began our inquiry, there was almost no systematic information on the impact of this process on either the students or the departments, or on the institution as a whole. The hidden curriculum grows like a giant weed in the well-cultivated educational garden. The analogy to the weed is limited, since the solution does not lie with pulling out the weed. However, we do need to inquire about the conditions of the soil and climate that nurture certain kinds of plants so well.

Many changes have occurred since 1961, when the study began. The tightly structured, interlocking set of stresses of the common first year has been loosened. The grading system has been altered so that now a freshman has pass/fail with specific comments from his faculty, and his professor has specific comments from his students on their educational encounter. In the early 1960's the stresses that the students met were qualitatively different from those they were to meet in subsequent years. At that time the first year forced an adaptive response in most students that, for many, carried through four years. This is even more striking since the nature of the stresses in the departments varied so; each had its *own* adaptation requirements.

The changes that were made came about in part because the institution was responsive to the knowledge that it began to gain of its impact on its students. Some of this came from the study; much came from direct communication between the faculty and students. The moral —if indeed there is one—would be the importance of developing reliable processes for change, for relevant feedback as the institution defines and examines its educational mission.[3]

A central task for an institution is to achieve a balance between openness and closure to stimuli: both the quality and quantity of stimuli (information techniques, etc.) to which the student must respond are obviously crucial to his education. A subtle, though somewhat less important, task for the student centers on his ability to remain open to new intellectual (and emotional) experiences while he is learning to neglect selectively certain parts of those experiences. In terms of the hidden curriculum some subjects, by virtue of their content and the way they are taught, require a high level of tolerance for ambiguity. Problems are open-ended, such as, How does a light bulb work? Assignments, in project laboratories especially, are largely determined by the students. This is in marked contrast to other subjects, where the student is required to schedule and organize his life in order to cover and memorize an extensive amount of material. The adaptive significance for the student of starting with his problem, his question, rather than someone else's, is profound. His investment in the outcome is real, not contrived.

One can locate the stresses in a university by the time

---

[3] For example, the Committee on Curriculum Content Planning, under Professor Jerrold R. Zacharias, reviewed the undergraduate curriculum in depth during 1961–3. Another example would be the shifts in departmental emphasis as a result of the changes in the fields.

at which they occur or by the geographical or social setting in which they seem to cluster. The point of the exercise is to build up a picture of the pressures in an institution so that one can begin to understand the adaptive patterns and the coping mechanisms required of individuals as they move through it.

I have just referred to the stresses in the first year at M.I.T. in 1961, particularly those imposed by the hidden curriculum's task of selective negligence. From the interviews and from the data on the movement of students across course boundaries and from withdrawal and disqualification rates, we discovered that the seventh semester appeared to present characteristic stresses that were qualitatively and quantitatively different from those occurring earlier. At another institution, at another time, the specifics would certainly vary, but the principle remains the same. Issues of career commitment and the impending separation from the institution lead many students to reexamine in the first term of their senior year their identity, their sense of who they are and who they are about to become. The climate in which this self-questioning occurs is crucial. In many colleges students are asking such questions by the end of freshman year or early in sophomore year. The initial loneliness of freshmen, the career crisis for faculty at the age of thirty-five or at the point of tenure, are further examples of stresses that are linked in part to the individual's age, the distance he has traveled along his own developmental path. But

THE HIDDEN CURRICULUM

they are also inextricably linked to the environment, to the opportunities for reflection or pressures to conform. The mastery of relativity theory, as noted earlier, presented a cognitive stress to students in sophomore physics in a setting where the grade was crucial. Whether they grasped the theory or were put down by it depended to a significant degree on the context in which they tried to learn it.

Having already in mind the question of the location of characteristic stresses, we examined the community's use of some of the "helping resources"—the Medical Department Outpatient Clinic and Infirmary, the Psychiatric Service, and the Dean's Office counseling staff. We reasoned that, if the stresses varied in the time they occurred and were also different for the various departments or in the several living groups (dorms, fraternities, apartments), the "rates of use"—the incidence—would vary depending on the particular path, since the stresses in each path would vary. The patterns of use of these resources did, in fact, vary among the departments and between the living groups. In one large department, 80 percent of the students consulting the psychiatrist came for the first time in their freshman year. In another department 78 percent came for the first time only when seniors. Approximately 80 percent of the students in one living group came into the Psychiatric Service in one semester. This did not become apparent until two years later, when the study of use patterns was undertaken. The majority

THE ECOLOGICAL TRAP

of the students from this living group felt some degree of depression and had largely defined their distress in personal terms. They, like the miners, had come complaining of "a cough." In retrospect, it is very likely that they were also responding to a social setting which was disruptive. The group was going through a crisis which affected the students' relationship to their education and clearly influenced their ability to function effectively in course work.

Some of the sudden stresses seemed to be connected with events and pressures that were essentially unrelated to the academic life of the institution—the effect, for example, of a destructively aggressive leader in a living group who left a trail of depressed classmates in his wake. But there was also a suggestion that the underlying stresses were located within the educational structure.

We came to the conclusion that most of the students using the Psychiatric Service were reasonably healthy individuals responding to dissonance in their immediate surroundings which threatened in some way their sense of worth and self-esteem. They came into what they perceived to be a relatively neutral arena, the Psychiatric Service, in order to sort out the mixed and contradictory signals that beset them. The clinical experience with this group could thus serve as a basis for posing questions about the impact of the environment, academic and other. It provided further documentation about the syllabus of the hidden curriculum and its effect on the choice of coping patterns made by students. Thus the Psychiatric Service and, to a considerable extent, all of those involved in helping individuals became, for the institution as a whole, a source of insight about some of the unexpected and unintended consequences of the immediate efforts of students to "fit in" with its overt and latent demands.

It should be emphasized that there are always a number of "filters" surrounding any helping resource which determine, in part, who will make use of it and under what circumstances. These filters clearly determine who will "volunteer" to seek help. For the Psychiatric Service the filters were the degree of confidentiality, availability, and accessibility. Beyond this, the psychiatrist's conception of his role, his notions of sickness and of cure, influenced the way he related to a student with an account of mild depression. Those physicians who focused exclusively on unconscious factors often ignored the present and were ignorant of their patients' adaptive crises.[4]

If the filters around the helping resource are minimal and are known to those working there, it is possible to study their use while protecting the individual's anonymity. The helping resources of an institution, particularly the counseling group but also the office secretary, the financial aid office, should ideally be so connected with the community that they can collectively provide a

[4] B. R. Snyder and M. J. Kahne: "Stress in Higher Education and Student Use of University Psychiatrists," *American Journal of Orthopsychiatry*, Vol. 39, No. 1 (Jan. 1969), pp. 23–35.

series of pictures about the effect of the environment on the lives that people lead within it. These "pictures" should be available to all participants. The helping resources can provide reasonably rapid feedback to the entire institution on the adaptive significance of the hidden curriculum. This is not its only function, clearly, nor can such understanding of the hidden curriculum come only from such data.

Student responses to the dissonance between the formal curriculum and the hidden curriculum vary from romanticism through cynicism to helplessness. The student who becomes cynical zeroes in on the immediate means of survival and does little serious examination of long-term goals and consequences. He spends his energy on "psyching" the professor. The romantic holds to an idealized view of his education and of his professors, many of whom are also romantics. The romantic solution for the faculty member is piecemeal reform—the "experimental seminar." This is a temporarily more comfortable position but is not a sound basis for long-term planning, for significant educational reform, or for significant educational experimentation.

The student who has begun to feel helpless, unable to decipher successfully the messages confronting him, has the most serious and dangerous response. His self-esteem will drop, and he will have less energy available to think through his dilemma and alter his circumstances. Since a certain number of this group will turn in their despair to one or more of the helping resources, it should be clear how crucial it is that any educational institution know not only about the individuals but also the trends of those who seek some help. It can then begin to seek out new supports and lower the level of dissonance where it is highest. Those who would help should not cool them out or use the label "sick" as a scapegoat.

The life history of each of us, with its particular developmental progressions, is lived out in a social structure which has its own rate of change, its own shifts in values and relevance. The pressures and the related supports built into a culture or a college may significantly affect the choices that individuals make at significant branching points in their life histories. If the pressures are too great (or not great enough), if the support structure is ineffective, then the development of the individual can come to a standstill; the energy needed for growth becomes, instead, used up in maintaining a defensive position. Such individuals have a hard time changing. The society which has sustained such outcomes is the loser.

The first step in coming to understand a student's response to his educational environment may indeed be to ask about the degree of his adjustment to a specific stress. However, the student and the institution must at least speculate about the long-term consequences of that adjustment to the individual student and the reciprocal effect on the college of the student's having, at whatever cost, fitted in. In this period of rapid social and technological change, educators and students will increasingly need to know far more than at present about the psychological and social means by which the students "adjust." Our survival a generation or two from now in some measure rests on our learning a great deal about the point at which an adjustment becomes irreversible, a cognitive style frozen.

7

EPILOGUE: WAYS OF KNOWING

Several years ago, while a participant-observer to a number of campus upheavals, I wrote the following account of a college in crisis. This is a composite drawn from my experience in six settings. My intent was not to expose any one institution but to recount what I saw in different institutions (one in Europe, several small, two large and state-supported). These institutions were responding with varying degrees of success to new pressures and demands with social and organizational structures, with patterns of decision-making that had been developed in response to quite different pressures in the past.

The student demonstrations were coming more frequently and their quality had changed. At first the whole campus had a festive air, but now that initial excitement had passed. The mild euphoria that drew the community perceptibly together at the first teach-in was gone, and with it the sense of involvement in the community itself. Everyone seemed to be "doing his own thing." Students

EPILOGUE: WAYS OF KNOWING

and faculty passed each other on the lawn in silence where before, a month ago, they would have smiled in passing.

The hard-core leaders were angry. Their following had diminished since the previous spring. Some had graduated or left school. Others had dropped out of the movement, having felt manipulated, "used," as much by their classmates as by the dean. Everyone was afraid of being "co-opted."

There had been some educational reforms over the preceding year; only one had been in response to student pressure. Feeling was running high over their merit. Several department chairmen felt threatened by the subsequent drop in enrollment in their no longer required subjects. Another department chairman, now overwhelmed with students, eyed his colleague's unused space and wondered aloud in a faculty committee about a reallocation in next year's departmental budgets.

The relatively easy pattern of life was gone, disrupted by increasingly frequent meetings that went on for hours and hours. There were faculty committees, joint student-faculty commissions, planning groups for the administration, for S.D.S. It was rarely that any of the participants could relate a tangible result to a particular investment of time. There was a sense of depletion, long hours, much debate, and no results. One student called it "Brownian movement."

A number of students sounded discouraged. They said in a hundred different ways that they felt unable to affect or influence the course of events, the outcome of issues that were important to them. Certainly the war, the draft came up repeatedly. Courses in English literature, in sociology, in political science as well as physics (though less so here) were seen as but a series of "precious" steps —one prerequisite to the other. But these students were asking: Where do these steps lead? They wanted to involve themselves and others (including often, their faculty) in real problems "out there."

A graduate student in science put it well.

> I've seen some very frustrated people who don't have the faith any longer that anybody can do anything about it. In fact, I have been sort of alarmed by that sort of thing, [and] even before finishing my Ph.D. have gotten involved in some of these urgent problems concerned with population and environment— . . . what man is doing to the world, . . . what technology has done to us without taking responsibility. I've been trying to convince people that there is something amiss here. People with brains are morally obliged to start looking at it. I encountered a lot of frustration because they would say, "You are wasting your time: . . . the world is going down the hatch; . . . there is nothing any of us can do about it."
>
> I'm afraid that among my friends I have already developed a reputation as too much of a crusader because I get rather worked up about this. It's their feeling that a scientist ought not to worry about things that aren't his province. In other words, these problems are largely political

EPILOGUE: WAYS OF KNOWING

problems, social problems. There are psychological considerations involved, and they say "What the hell do you know if you are a plasma physicist or an aeronautical engineer?" My opinion is that any intelligent man confronted with a complicated situation looks at it, analyzes it the best he can, and then decides what to do about it. If you just don't look at it or don't decide, you are "copping out." As I say, I get some gas about this from my friends for writing papers and giving talks.

The conditions for feeling good about themselves had changed for a number of students. The old rewards and the supports were becoming the object of suspicion, of attack, of ridicule. The dean of students and the guidance counselor were more and more seen as "company men" employed to keep the restless natives quiet. Most students liked the men involved but saw them as having to keep the lid on, "cooling out" (counseling out) those students who did not accept the educational status quo. The students said this was their role whether they knew it or not.

The faculty had begun to form into separate camps, not yet armed. Some spoke with sadness, some with bitterness, about the way their time was no longer their own. They too were mildly depressed and spoke of their inability to order their daily lives the way they had done a year before. As the meetings continued, arguments flared over changes in curriculum, over grades, over the proper response to student demonstrations. Hard and soft attitudes formed; pressure was brought on those still uncommitted to take sides. There were other sides—tenure and nontenure faculty members, young and old. There was no clear division, however, along academic lines.

The president had recovered from the shock of a week before when fifty students, waving banners and beating drums, had come into his office unannounced. They stayed for twenty minutes, presented their demands, and left. They had been very rude. The president thought they took delight in using only four-letter words. He felt they had wanted to provoke him; he had barely managed to keep his anger under control; he wanted to keep from "losing his cool" so that the communication channel to the other students might stay at least partly open. He had avoided calling the police. They would have cleared his office their own way and he would, he said, have lost all semblance of control of the situation. Television and radio, the press, frantic calls from alumni, trustees, and angry citizens were part of his peripheral vision as he decided to wait this one out. He saw his immediate task as maintaining maximum room in which to maneuver between the various groups. As the semester wore on, he felt a creeping discouragement; he had lost his easy optimism. His "kitchen cabinet" of top administration and some faculty members continued to huddle over drinks in the evening and spent their time trying to guess what tomorrow's crisis would be. He knew that time and energy

EPILOGUE: WAYS OF KNOWING

were limited, that all this putting out of bonfires meant that the momentum for what he called constructive educational reform was being dissipated at the barricades.

Trustees flew in for hurried consultation. While deference was still shown them, they were more like ministers without portfolio, troubled by the pattern of events; and some, for the first time in their lives, were unable to predict with confidence where events might lead. Others were certain in their knowledge of the proper remedy. They had their private scapegoats and urged the president to act against them.

So there was little playfulness and no kidding on the campus. Conversations began seriously, became acrimonious, and ended in anger. The sense of helplessness touched all participants from students to trustees. Many, indeed most, handled this mildly depressed mood by holding ever more tightly to their point of view.

As the semester progressed, positions polarized. Each group became increasingly preoccupied with conspiratorial explanations for the other's outrageous or insidious behavior. The growing distrust eroded the usual channels of communication and undercut the sense of worth that had come from knowing that one's colleagues respected and cared about each other.

The polarized positions gradually froze. Although it appeared to some that this happened suddenly, following a demonstration that "went too far" (a member of the faculty attacked the dean in senate for his handling of the episode), the freeze had actually begun in earnest a month before, when petitions had been passed around for all members of the community to sign. "Now you can see who your friends are," was the comment of a young professor. The college was like a supersaturated solution; all it took was one more crystal and some slight shaking of the glass before the solution became a solid mass. Communication on the pressing and central educational matters had broken down. These issues were now cast in political terms and negotiated like a labor relations contract. The communication network, the shared experiences, the trust that had previously sustained a dialogue, had faded. Each group now negotiated from its own position, giving ground only to move the adversary farther from its stance.

The campus was no longer a setting where assumptions could be openly, genuinely examined. Assumptions were only attacked. Simpler and simpler explanations were being offered by almost all participants for the still unrecognized crises. Scapegoating became the order of the day—whether S.D.S., black militants, the administration, or a piece of college-held real estate. The explanations heard at faculty cocktail parties were the same as those heard in late night bull sessions in the dorm. Only the names of the actors changed.

The issues were not illusory but real; their merit, however, depended on their viewer's perspective. Independent of their merit, these issues had come to serve as

EPILOGUE: WAYS OF KNOWING

lightning rods for the general frustration, the malaise that gripped the whole community. In the end, the central failure of education on campus was ignored, and in this sense these other issues were scapegoating.

There are lessons to be drawn from this scenario. The depression, the distrust, the dehumanization affected all participants. Rage smoldered just beneath the surface. One leader invoked the message of Martin Luther King—nonviolence and love—as justification for breaking down a door, for smashing an objet d'art. His rhetoric, in which all means justified his ends, did violence to King's nonviolence. (The rhetoric from the political right was almost identical, only the content differed.) An early and serious casualty of the crisis was language. It had been debased; words shifted in some strange manner so that the signal embedded in a sentence had to be read in an unaccustomed context. Individuals were transformed into icons by the abuse of language. The icons then became the target of the anger and were attacked—or alternatively—revered and worshiped.

There is great danger for students, parents, faculty members, and politicians when we come to rely on simple models of the world of human beings in order to explain how things work, how education educates, how and why students learn. There was a time when societies were stable over centuries and when such simple formulations were adequate to the task of sustaining decisions and choices about human events. Now it is all far more complex. Events and technologies have surged ahead so fast that what was relevant for our generation may have almost no relevance for the next. The simple view (that of Adam Smith or the romantic nineteenth-century revolutionary) that has outlived its relevance, its power to adequately inform decisions, can be quaint, romantic, or even grotesque. The individual who holds tightly to his model of the world becomes furious at anyone who points out that events have changed, that his mode no longer works. He characteristically looks outside himself, not within, to find an explanation for the failure of his views. In this circumstance he cannot adapt to the new situation that confronts him. He begins to seek a scapegoat on which to vent his anger. One of the more likely scapegoats will be the individual who raises questions and challenges simple formulations, who suggests that the context has altered. The man who thinks that the complications will be simplified if the questioner is attacked or the context ignored loses the opportunity to know, to grow, to change, whether he stands to the right or left. This is the dilemma and one of the principal dangers facing education in America today.

The crisis in education is broader and deeper than the immediate problems encountered in elite American institutions with their able students. Their problems, important in their own right, are symptomatic of a system in profound difficulty. Alienation, helplessness, and unrest occur in universities in Spain, in Hungary, in France, in Japan, nations where the Vietnamese war cannot be invoked as primary cause. The war and the black revolt are symptomatic of a global disregard for the conservation of our physical, social, and psychological resources. Our system of education, with all its expertise and its compartmentalization of knowledge, has largely failed to alert us sufficiently to the probable consequences of our present course. In those countries and those universities that I know at all well, the hidden curriculum functions as insulation for the formal curriculum, focusing the attention of students and faculties on the measures for immediate academic survival. And so the liberal arts curriculum remains largely divorced from science; past historical or economic trends are not projected into the future but become an end in themselves. Higher education has been principally concerned with the development and cultivation of impressive, often beautiful, sometimes useful, sometimes precious models of pieces of experience. So we in higher education have built our separate models of our corner of the world, in mathematics, sociology, psychoanalysis, physics, literary criticism.

These models form the basis of the formal curriculum. Mastery of these models has come to be the measure of our students' minds. The hidden curriculum has ironically protected these models of the formal curriculum from our students' skepticism. Serious confrontation between these curricula has so far been delayed. Accommodation to the educational status quo continues to be the principal adaptive mode of all participants. And in the meantime, to paraphrase the young professor quoted in Chapter 1, the world may be going down the drain around us. How could a generation or more of academics (and many generations of students) fail for so long to see what was happening?

I have used the metaphor of the ecological trap, the analogy of the lemmings, to dramatize the consequences of misreading the nature of the balance of a species—man—with its environment. By focusing on short-term survival, we have dangerously limited our vision and our perspective.

The effect of the educational environment on the lives of the students and the faculty extends far beyond the classroom. The actual relationships between student and faculty, either close or impersonal, influence in a number of specific ways the basis for each individual's self-esteem. We have seen some of the ways in which this happens. Let us also consider two contrasting qualities of communication, two different predominant modes of communication between faculty, administration, and students.

Negotiation is a means of coming to terms, a conferring with the aim of arriving at a basis for agreement. The word is derived from Latin *negotium*, which means "business"; originally it meant "absence of leisure." The most important point in the context of this discussion is

EPILOGUE: WAYS OF KNOWING

that negotiation does not presuppose trust between the parties doing business; at least, the degree of trust can be limited and the areas of disagreement large. Those involved in negotiation start from prepared positions and usually give ground as it serves their essentially political ends. Negotiation then actually limits choices and narrows the range of action between negotiating parties. This is what some of the students seem to be asking for. They make the claim that the university is essentially a political structure and for them to be expected to ignore this is the first step to their being co-opted. The quality of communication between individuals who are negotiating, who see themselves in a political interaction, has significant implications for the verbal, the cognitive, and even the life style that the negotiator develops. I am primarily concerned here with the implications of such a mode for an educational institution. The issue can be sharpened best by comparing negotiation briefly with dialogue.

Dialogue means "conversation." In this context it is a colloquy with the use of reason and follows rules of logic. Dialogue is intended to explore the area under discussion, in direct contrast to negotiation, where the intent is to limit the area of discussion and narrow the range of choice.[1]

---

[1] A third possibility is now emerging on many campuses which differs from both negotiation and dialogue. It is anti-intellectualism. In a profound sense it is a denial of dialogue and negotiation precisely because they both have rules. There is a suspicion on the part of a number

A precondition of dialogue is at least sufficient trust between the participants to permit them to expose their reasoning to critical review and to reexamine that reasoning in themselves. There is an assumption, shared by the participants, that through such an exercise some closer approximation to "truth" will be possible. The personal relationships, the interactions between the participants in a dialogue differ dramatically from the relationship between the parties to negotiation. Another condition for successful dialogue is freedom from fear and a willingness to expose oneself and to explore. Where there is fear of exposing oneself or of exploring, negotiation is likely to be the mode. If negotiation rather than dialogue should become the major mode of communication at an educational institution, the latent tasks and the patterns for validating one's sense of worth will be very different, even though the academic tasks of the formal curriculum may look identical before and after. The crucial difference can be expected to lie in the hidden curriculum, in the psychological and cognitive styles that lead to success, as defined in that particular institution. Where negotiation has become the means by which students communicate with the faculty or with the administration, there has been a covert, but nonetheless critical, break in trust and shared

of students and some others that logic leaves out the unexpected, the poetic, the emotional. They seek other ways of knowing: the media, encounter groups, drugs, the happening. This third approach sets in motion a process without any necessary fixed idea of where it may lead or how it may end.

EPILOGUE: WAYS OF KNOWING

assumptions. Where negotiation is the mode, there is a strong suggestion that the tasks to which the faculty and the administration are committed are not considered crucial by the students. The assumptions underlying both the formal and the hidden curriculum are not shared, nor are these differences openly discussed and mutually explored. There are possible hazards for both the students and the faculty in such a setting.

I am reminded of the impressive, careful, clinical work of Stanton and Schwartz[2] in their study of the mental hospital. They described a situation in which patients in an essentially closed society, a ward of a mental hospital, became pathologically hyperactive in response to a breakdown in communication between their doctors or other significant individuals who were responsible for them. The patients' physicians were not communicating with each other directly about their differences in their view of what was best for the patients. These covert disagreements were transmitted, however, to and through the patient as if he were both a telephone wire and a puppet. The patients found themselves in great difficulties and began to oscillate between the various positions that their doctors took. They then became excited and manic and started to scream. Their screams against such instrumental use were diagnosed by the physicians as illness. Calling

---

[2] Alfred H. Stanton and Morris S. Schwartz: *The Mental Hospital: A Study of Institutional Participation in Psychiatric Illness and Treatment* (New York: Basic Books; 1954).

the screaming or agitation illness was both poor medicine and self-deception. Stanton and Schwartz showed that when the physicians finally communicated directly about their disagreement and clarified the issue among themselves instead of through the patient, the patient in each instance was no longer hyperactive and his screaming ceased.

Negotiation may well help to resolve the dilemma for the doctors and thus for the patient by at least establishing the need for new channels of communication. However, there is some risk that negotiation in the setting of the hospital may trap the doctors further in their unacknowledged fight and leave the patient caught between them. A dialogue, and by this I mean essentially a climate which would sustain a dialogue, would prevent the trap from developing in the first place.

There is much here that is instructive for the university. The extent to which all members of the academic community are genuinely willing and able to involve themselves with the educational tasks and to put their own self-esteem on that line will be a function, to a significant degree, of the trust in and alliance with the people around them. This is quite a burden to put on education, educators, and students. It is no simple task to work out the logistics of providing the conditions for a dialogue in a university. However, such conditions have at least as much influence on fundamental attitudes of faculty, students, and administration toward each other as do the

EPILOGUE: WAYS OF KNOWING

actual numbers of students in a classroom or the priorities of research versus teaching. These latter issues, rather, are likely to be reflections of the underlying attitudes. If the possibility for a dialogue, as I have defined the term, is lost, then the universities as we know them will not survive.

When negotiation is the principal means of communication in an educational institution, the essential humanness of the interaction between the negotiating parties may well be denied. Both of the negotiating parties become more vulnerable in a special sense. They may hold more tightly to their own frame of reference, to their own model of the situation, and ignore the complexity of the context in which they are operating. The possibilities for mixed messages, for double binds like those described in the mental hospital, greatly increases. The negotiators, whether faculty, administrators, or students, force their frame of reference rather than examine it. This re-examination is vital in an educational institution.

There are other hazards for the negotiator beyond his tendency to stereotype, to studiously avoid feelings that might upset the balance of his discourse or affect his pre-established system of priorities. If negotiation is the only way a college administration or a group of faculty members or a group of students will listen to each other, then there has been a serious breakdown in communication and in trust. To stop and say, as some of the doctors did of their hyperactive patients, that the students or the administrators are sick, obscures—even as it did for the hospital—what is not working in the larger system of which they both are a part.

There is a further possible consequence for the negotiator who is successful in this mode of communication. The complaint of many student negotiators is that they are caught in a system which is cold and bureaucratic. The irony is that precisely such individuals may develop their own impersonal ways of dealing with one another and become manipulators of men at the expense of intimacy.

There is an urgent need for significant educational reform and, beyond that, for educational innovation or experiment in colleges and universities. The way in which individuals determine which aspects of education warrant reform is of a different intellectual order from that of generating educational innovations and experiments. Once the determination of what to reform is made, the strategies and tactics appropriate to implementing those structural reforms will almost certainly be different from those appropriate to the implementation of an educational experiment. Reforms may well have to be negotiated between various academic departments or in faculty committees or with student groups.

Certain necessary, though not in themselves sufficient, conditions must obtain in the educational climate of any institution before many types of experiments have even a minimal chance of success. Experiment is not a variety of reform and may even be the opposite—a substitute for reform. It may be that some reforms are prerequisite to any significant educational experiment. Some aspects of departmental structure may cut against an integrated approach to problem areas such as interdisciplinary courses in air pollution or arms control. The real constraints are vested departmental interests and traditional assumptions and values. Thus the first task facing the professor or the student experimenter is to determine the basic limiting factors in the system with which he has to deal and whether they may have to be changed. However, in any system, old or new, there will be some limiting factors acting on an experiment, and to ignore them is to court failure.

Notions about reform derive from a view of what is a proper order, of what is morally best or better, and thus what constitutes a "vicious habit" to be reformed. In an educational institution, these notions are directly related to our models of the student, the teacher, and the learning process. The issue is complicated by the fact that these notions are most often held as implicit assumptions, embedded in the hidden curriculum, and thus not easily subject to direct examination. The reformer's assumptions often have to be inferred from his language, his style, and his program. The reformer often seeks consensus and then action (or action followed by consensus!) by an appeal to the emotions, though he may well use reason and logic as his means to this end. An educational institution dedicated to the experimental method should be especially alert to the danger of considerable dissonance in the system if a reform is presented as an experiment or an experiment as a structural reform.

I have stated my concern for the educational and psychological consequences of the acceleration in the rate of technological and scientific progress, for the increasing impact of science and engineering on the lives we lead and the society we live in. The society is also changing. Social roles, once unambiguous and relevant, are becoming more peripheral and cloudy to the holder of the role and the society itself. In 1900 a civil engineer built bridges; today he may be an expert in computers, managing a research and development company that is trying to design a transport system through a ghetto in a manner that its residents will accept. A minister in 1900 knew the value of hard work as revealed by Calvin; not long ago I saw a pastor in Berkeley wearing a beard and beads and talking of touching his congregation as the new Communion.

My own response to this rapid change has been to move toward a position between reform and experiment by taking the hypotheses generated in the research and developing programs that might implement them rather than rigorously test them. This seems to be legitimate if the experiment meets at least three conditions:

First, the entire institution—the administration, the faculty, the students—must be able to learn relatively

EPILOGUE: WAYS OF KNOWING

quickly and with reasonable ease whether the experiment has succeeded or failed, in general and in the specific case. If a sociology course in group behavior is designed to encourage some taking of cognitive risk, exploration of the limits of the student's competence, rather than instrumental gamesmanship and a playback on the quiz of the student's perception of the professor's wish, we need to know at least the consensus of all the participants on just these dimensions.

Second, if an experiment fails, after the whys of the failure have been approximately determined, it should be possible to drop the experiment and avoid its being institutionalized. Some experiments are of such a size and involve such an institutional investment in money, time, and self-esteem that it may seem virtually impossible to cut them off without tearing the institution apart. A voyage of discovery in an educational institution should be preceded by sufficient, careful navigation to fix the point of departure and the approximate arrival position; though in a time of rapid change a line of position and a possibility of taking fixes at intervals may be enough to plot a course and avoid a reef if conditions change. A local weather report will tell us little of what we most need to know about the day after tomorrow; it holds only for this morning or this afternoon. So there is the obvious danger that caution over campus politics may forestall any movement.

Third, resources of time and personnel and probably of money are limited, so that a trivial experiment should not be given a higher priority than more salient experiments that may touch on and illuminate central educational concerns. Trivial experiments expend the institution's energy, fritter away the relatively small resources for innovation, and lead in time to a generally shared sense of helplessness about the possibility of effective change. This is the most difficult condition to discuss because it is here that the roles of researcher and reformer are likely to merge.

It may prejudice the reader to use such words as "trivial" or "salient." But to change the number of students in a recitation section from twenty to ten and to change nothing else would be a trivial experiment. Further, it would be naïve, for it would leave untouched for most students their reliance on grades for their self-esteem. Most professors would continue to focus on quizzes; and, if they did not, most of their students would soon bring them into line or cut the class.

If we start with the hypothesis that students might be motivated primarily from within to search for the limits of their knowledge of a field instead of being motivated by a high grade-point average, it would mean that they must become competent in the specifics of their discipline in order to find out what they do not know, not to show what they do know. The limits of the field could well include, for example, both the current mathematical models used in physics and the possible social consequences of those models when applied to technology. This shift could profoundly alter what the student would eagerly expose of his misunderstanding of the course to his teacher-colleague, instead of carefully hiding his uncertainties about its content from his quiz-oriented mentor. To use the rhetoric of the reformer, the basis for the student's self-esteem might then shift from grade to wonder.

We can speculate on the institutional changes necessary to bring about such a shift in values and in motivation and the quality of learning. It would mean a very different use of the time spent between the student and the professor, though it is by no means evident that it would mean substantially more time. Much program learning, the use of project labs, package pieces of the curriculum could provide the student with an opportunity to acquire the basic competences in sociology, French grammar, or Newtonian mechanics. While this still has to be demonstrated, let us say for the sake of argument that it is possible. The student and the professor together would determine the progress of the student in his understanding of certain central concepts in his discipline. This would require trust between the student and the professor and the relative absence in both of shame in acknowledging their relative ignorance, not at the beginning but at the end of their encounter. Given this set of aspirations, everything—lectures, recitations, grades, even living arrangements—takes on a new significance and relevance. Such a shift in focus would not be trivial and might move us somewhat closer to educating students who appreciate the meaning of cognitive obsolescence, the danger of an arrogantly held scientific or moral position. Both the student and professor would appreciate the meaning of the hidden curriculum.

The implementation of such a program in many universities would run hard aground on departmental requirements, on grading practices, on the sanctions on the faculty's time and interests, and on the differences between the student's own image of his current education and that of his faculty—in short, on the hidden curriculum.

There are many students whose energy and enthusiasm from their earliest years to those of graduate school have been constrained by learning to fit in with our educational system. The hidden curriculum in American schools in the 1960's may have erred on this side. In other settings and at other times, the absence of constraints may have been the problem. For example, thirty years ago the excesses of progressive education often called for limits. However, today's education has far too frequently contained rather than freed the minds of students while they have been diligently acquiring concepts and skills (which in fact they would most certainly need but also need to question). These academically able students have taken few intellectual risks or explored few alternatives as they developed their special skills. The educa-

EPILOGUE: WAYS OF KNOWING

tional system rewarded them with A's, with scholarships, with admission to an "elite," precisely because they adjusted so well to their assigned tasks. The hidden curriculum has taught students that the material and immediate rewards go with conforming to the way things are done on a campus or in the classroom (or in the society outside). The "payoff" in terms of grades and scholarships on many campuses has come to the student who avoided rather than took some intellectual risk with the formal curriculum, with the prescribed syllabus. The grading system in most of our educational institutions is seldom organized with the intention of penalizing the students' curiosity, though it has often this effect by judging performance on a very discrete set of prescribed skills and ignoring the students' restless curiosity. The danger of obsolescence for the student who so adjusts has been the central concern of this book.

In the hidden curriculum words have been used in defense of the indefensible: "creativity" has become the cover for "conformity"; "adaptation" has become "niceness of fit." The result has been euphemism and a very dangerous vagueness in the meaning of words. The custodial function of education has been glossed over. This function has been explained in terms that becloud the issue—at a time when the challenge is man's survival. The words have blurred the outlines of the details instead of defining them. The insincerity of the formal curriculum has been obscured by an evasion, an erosion in the meaning of words. In this atmosphere, education has suffered, and the hidden curriculum has flourished.

This debasement of language is a symptom of the debasement of education. The politics of the right and of the left bear a significant responsibility for this outcome, though liberal education bears the primary responsibility. Education, instead of developing and expressing thought, has come all too often to conceal and prevent thought.

All this leads to a further strain on the system. Disillusionment, alienation, or gamesmanship has become the context in which increasing numbers of students view their education. The specifics of the hidden curriculum may remain the same on a given campus. Today's students see its syllabus in a very different context from that of even a decade or half a decade ago. The context and content of the formal curriculum, as well as the hidden curriculum, must be the subject of a searching dialogue if higher education is to have any relevance at all in the coming decades.

A NOTE ABOUT THE AUTHOR

Benson R. Snyder is Dean for Institute Relations at Massachusetts Institute of Technology. Born in Glen Ridge, New Jersey, in 1923, he was educated at Bard College, the University of Pennsylvania, and New York University, where he received his M.D. in 1948. He has been a resident at Cincinnati General Hospital, a fellow in the Department of Psychiatry at Beth Israel Hospital in Boston, and a graduate of the Boston Psychoanalytic Institute. He served in the Air Force, 1951–3. In 1954, Dr. Snyder began a private practice of psychotherapy in Boston, also teaching at various hospitals in the area and acting as consulting psychiatrist to Wellesley College until 1959. That year he became psychiatrist-in-chief at M.I.T., and in 1967 was appointed Professor of Psychiatry at the institute. In 1969, Dr. Snyder accepted his present position. He has worked on various boards and commissions at the National Institutes of Health, the Peace Corps, and the Office of Science and Technology, and has contributed many articles to professional journals. He is a trustee of Antioch College. The father of six children, Dr. Snyder lives in Wellesley Hills, Massachusetts.

A NOTE ON THE TYPE

The text of this book was set in CALEDONIA, a Linotype face designed by W. A. Dwiggins. It belongs to the family of printing types called "modern face" by printers—a term used to mark the change in style of type letters that occurred about 1800. Caledonia borders on the general design of Scotch Modern, but is more freely drawn than that letter. This book was composed, printed, and bound by The Colonial Press Inc., Clinton, Mass. Typography and binding design by Constance T. Doyle.